'The one duty we owe to history is to rewrite it.'
(Oscar Wilde)

ACKNOWLEDGEMENTS

They say that writing is a lonely job, but in my case, I have never felt alone.
Andreas, Costas and Mona were the first to suggest to put in writing all the findings that I was making. During the whole process they have always been there for me.
There were countless people that listened to all my stories while I was getting my thoughts in order.
Bonny and Adrian, without knowing, have given me tools that have made the whole process a lot easier.
Dan whose expert advice shaped the book to what it is today.
Zach who designed the book cover, and has always been there helping me.
Finally, the Paphos Writers Group who have been there right from the beginning. Especially, John, Bob and Nikki who have supported and guided me for the last ten years. Without their help none of this would have ever happened.

Thank you all.

Special Thanks to the Department of Antiquities who supplied the images of the artifacts exhibited in the Cyprus Museum.

Jordi Guri Harth ©
Jordi Guri Harth asserts the moral right
to be identified as the author of this work.

First publication June 2024.

A catalogue record for this book is available from the Cyprus Library.
CIP 939.37–dc23   20240522

All rights reserved. No part of this publication may be reproduced, stored in a retrieval system, or transmitted, in any form or by any means, electronic, mechanical, photocopying, recording or otherwise, without the prior permission of the author.

Website: jordiguriharth.com
Email: jordiguriharth@outlook.com

Cover design: Zacharias Archontous
Cover Image: https://creativemarket.com/Sotnikov_Misha/6160058-Peaceful-bright-beach-seaside
Interior layout: Creative Madness Studio

ISBN 978-9925-8131-0-0

CONTENTS

Introduction		7
Chapter 1	| The Origin of Civilization	23
Chapter 2	| Atlantean Geography	43
Chapter 3	| The Island of the Gods	65
Chapter 4	| Troy and Homer	85
Chapter 5	| Atlantean Army	101
Chapter 6	| The Legacy of Atlantis	117
Conclusion		157
Bibliography		163
Endnotes		169

INTRODUCTION

Cyprus, crossroad of civilizations. Situated at the eastern end of the Mediterranean Sea, right between Africa, Asia and Europe. Its strategic location made it the ideal meeting point for the world's greatest civilizations and the ideal venue for trade, not just in goods but also technology and ideas. As a result, this little island became one of the most culturally and technologically advanced places in the ancient world. But, as good as that sounds, it also made it one of the most sought-after conquests in antiquity. All civilizations wanted to have Cyprus under their control. Over thousands of years Cyprus was invaded time after time. Looking back through the nation's history, we can see the reason why Cypriots are so resilient to unrest. Cypriots have drawn the short straw for more than 3,000 years.

In the 8th century BC, they were overrun by the Assyrian Empire, which took charge of the island and imposed special taxes. All rebellions were crushed. In the 6th century BC, the same thing happened with the Egyptians. After the Egyptians, the Persians invaded. Whole cities were destroyed for not following the orders of these foreign rulers. The period after Alexander the Great (356–323 BC) and his descendants might have been the only instance in which Cypriots enjoyed more peaceful and prosperous times, but it didn't last. The Romans invaded in 58 BC and they would stay until the split of the Roman Empire into east and west in 395 AD. In the year 117 AD Cyprus suffered, as many other areas did, a Jewish rebellion in which, in Cyprus alone, more than 240,000 Romans and Cypriots were killed.[1] After that, not many people would have been left on the island. The Roman repression of the revolt was very rigorous; any Jew was to be killed if he was ever to set foot on the island again, even if they had been shipwrecked off the Cyprus coast.[2]

After the fall of the Roman Empire, the Byzantines ruled the island. In the year 649 the Arabs invaded. Byzantines and Arabs did not agree on many things, but one thing they agreed on was the benefit of ruling Cyprus. So badly did each want this power that, while they were fighting each other on the mainland, they agreed to jointly rule Cyprus. This arrangement would last for another 300 years. The only people not benefiting from the agreement were, of course, the indigenous Cypriots.

In 1155, crusader Raynald of Châtillon made an unprovoked attack on the island, which was described by William of Tyre:

'He sent forth his legions as against enemy and laid violent hands on Cyprus, the neighboring island which had always been useful and friendly to our realm and which had a large population of Christians.'[3]

He continued:

'For several days Renaud's forces continued to ravage the whole country and, since there was none to offer resistance, they showed no mercy to age or sex, neither did they recognize difference of condition. Finally, laden with a vast amount of riches and spoils of every kind, they returned to the seashore. When the ships were ready, they embarked and set sail for Antioch..[4]

INTRODUCTION

Less than 30 years later, in 1184, Isaac Komnenos, a self-proclaimed emperor, seized control of Cyprus, and began to exert his power. Unfortunately for Komnenos, King Richard I of England, the Lionheart, arrived and took the island by storm. The islanders felt like they had been liberated, but the feeling did not last. Richard sold the island to the Knights Templar, and a rebellion ensued. Cypriots became so unruly that the Templars returned the rule to Richard I, who then sold the country to the king of Jerusalem. The island changed hands yet again in 1489 (to Venice) and again in 1570 (to the Ottomans). Despite an unsuccessful attempt by a loose coalition of Catholic states (including Spain and Venice), urged by the pope into action, Cyprus would remain under Ottoman rule until 1878. During those years, Cypriots were oppressed yet again, this time by taxation from their new rulers. Non-Muslims became, in effect, second-class citizens.

After the Russo-Turkish war the Berlin congress decided that Cyprus would be leased to the British. In 1915 England offered the islands to the Greeks on condition of joining their side on World War I. When the Greeks said no, the British arranged for Cyprus to become officially a British colony. It would not be until 1960 that Cyprus finally acquired its independence from the British. Even then, hidden forces among the Greek and Turkish communities of Cyprus started confronting each other, and a civil war began. In 1974, with the pretext of protecting the Cypriot Turkish community, the Turkish army invaded and took control of a third of the island. Cyprus has remained a divided country ever since. Following the fall of the Berlin Wall, amidst media frenzy, Nicosia became the only capital in the world where a wall still divides the city, a fact much of the world's media continues to ignore.

In addition to the political, economic and cultural upheavals, over millennia Cypriots have had to endure geological upheavals, which have also played a major role in the island's history. Cyprus was born out of the colliding tectonic plates of Europe, Asia and Africa, which pushed the island upwards, giving it the magnificent mountain ranges of Troodos and Pentadaktylos. But, as much as a blessing, this has also been a curse for Cyprus, as time after time the island has suffered from destructive earthquakes.

In 26 BC the area of Paphos was struck by a very strong earthquake. In 76 AD another quake virtually destroyed Paphos, Kition, and Salamis. Evidence suggests that nearly every 100 years there has been major destruction in the cities on the southern coast of the island. If that was not enough, in many cases there is evidence of major tsunamis following the earthquakes. In 1222 AD, a bishop and the whole congregation died when the cathedral collapsed. The scene was described by Ogerius Panis:

'the sea rose from the quake and dashed to the shore; huge volumes of seawater, large as mountains, flooded the coast, demolishing buildings and filling the villages with fish. Paphos, they say, suffered the most ... the harbour dried and the city was flooded by the sea; the city and the castle were destroyed and the residents disappeared ....'[15]

Earthquakes and tsunamis occurred so often that they were a common prediction in ancient oracles. In Oracula Sibyllina from the second or third century, we read:

'Then an earthquake will destroy Salamis and Paphos together, when the black water rushes over sea-girt Cyprus.'[16]

'Delos, you will float and become unstable in water. Cyprus, a wave of your wedded sea will destroy you.'[17]

If that was not enough, Cyprus has also suffered pestilence, plague, droughts, floods, and many other calamities. Yet all is not as gloomy as it looks. During the period from the first arrival of settlers on the island until the end of the Bronze Age, Cyprus was the global leader in developments. According to ancient writers, the Cypriot kings were the richest in the world. But the greatest era in Cyprus's history has long been written off as mere legend. In this book, I will argue that Cyprus was, in fact, a long-forgotten superpower – the centre of a mighty empire according to Plato. It was the centre of the lost civilization of Atlantis. The idea of an empire with Cyprus at its centre seems so unreal now as it was during Plato's time. It probably was the reason why Plato felt the need to start his story with:

> 'Then listen, Socrates, to a tale which, though strange,
> is certainly true.'

Deciphering Plato's Writings

Around 360 BC, Plato, one of the most respected persons in antiquity, wrote two dialogues called Critias and Timaeus. In these texts, he describes an island he called Atlantis. The texts unfortunately are incomplete, and researchers have struggled ever since to discover the true location of the elusive island.

Today, we still do not have a theory that matches Plato's description and is accompanied by the prerequisite archaeological remains. Many locations seemed likely but failed to produce any verifiable artefacts. Other sites held promising remains yet did not match Plato's description of the island.

People have been looking for Atlantis without success for many years, so many years that we have come to doubt the veracity of the story. There are many theories about what Plato could have meant by relating the story of Atlantis—but it must be noted that Plato showed no interest in science fiction in any of his other writings. The story of Atlantis is, according to Plato, the story of an island that led the developments that birthed human civilization. It is the story of a place where humans became what we are now; a place with the most advanced technology of its time, a structured society, with highly developed political systems. And all this happened, according to Plato, 9,000 years before his time.

Literature and films have created a distorted image of how Atlantis should appear. Scenes with submerged palaces—all intact and looking as though they were constructed yesterday—are far from reality. We have seen first-hand, as recently as 2004 Indian Ocean or 2011 in Fukushima, the devastation that tsunamis and earthquakes can cause. In addition, we have seen the effects of the ravages of time on archaeological sites. Atlantis, once found, would look like most other sites from the same period. Greek temples are approximately 2,500 years old and now stand only as ruins. It is unreasonable to believe that a site thousands of years older would look exactly the same today as it did before it was submerged.

Another issue is that the story of Atlantis comes only from secondary sources. The original texts by Plato have been translated numerous times, leading to countless errors. Worse, Plato suggests in Timaeus that there might have been some mistakes in his recollection of details due to the excessive passage of time since he'd heard the story:

'For a long time had elapsed, and I had forgotten too much; I thought that I must first of all run over the narrative in my own mind, and then I would speak.'

One can also deduce that the 'telephone' or 'Chinese whispers' effect might have affected the story, as Plato himself alludes to in Timaeus: *'He was a relative and a dear friend of my great-grandfather, Dropides, as he himself says in many passages of his poems; and he told the story to Critias, my grandfather, who remembered and repeated it to us.'*

'I will tell an old-world story which I heard from an aged man; for Critias, at the time of telling it, was, as he said, nearly ninety years of age, and I was about ten.'

Clearly a story that Critias had not heard first-hand and was told when he was ten years old might have become a little distorted. Mistakes made in early interpretations have been carried through time, and we seem to take for granted things that should not be.

The Real Atlantis

One thing we can take for granted, though, is that Atlantis really did exist. In Timaeus, Plato tells Socrates:

'Then listen, Socrates, to a tale which, though strange, is certainly true, having been attested by Solon, who was the wisest of the seven sages.'

Once the story has been told, they checked the suitability of the story for the festival of the goddess and Socrates was left to decide if the story was to be used. He then replied:

'And what other, Critias, can we find that will be better than this, which is natural and suitable to the festival of the goddess, and has the very great advantage of being a fact and not a fiction.'

To Plato there was never any doubt that the story related was nothing but the truth. One of his disciples, Crantor of Soli, took the time to travel to Egypt to verify the story. He was actually shown by the priest at Sais a pillar with hieroglyphs telling the story of the sinking of Atlantis. In Plato's time, there was no doubt that Atlantis was very real.

But, as often happens, what once was very real to most people now seems unbelievable. Atlantis non-believers have been trying for centuries to disprove all the theories put forward by the believers.

So far, the non-believers have had the upper hand as none of the proposed locations seemed to completely add up. Some of the theories put forward include the following.

Crete

When the remains of the Minoan civilization were discovered in Crete, some people linked them to the lost island. The buildings of the Palace at Knossos resemble the ones described by Plato, since they were built on many levels, have intricate water piping systems, and were earthquake resistant. In fact, this technology was unheard of in mainland Greece until much later.

However, the Palace of Knossos was built on the Kephala hill on top of a settlement dating back to 7000 BC, and its ruins still rest about 100 metres above sea level. There is no evidence that it ever sank into the sea. Also, the disappearance of the Minoan society happened around 1400 BC, a period when no major conflict occurred in the area. Crete has similarly failed to produce any remains of the temples to Poseidon mentioned by Plato. While the Minoans were a very advanced society and their cities appear to resemble what the city of Atlantis would have looked like, the island of Crete simply doesn't fit the ancient descriptions we have of Atlantis.

Santorini

Excavations on the island of Santorini revealed that there were Minoans on that island too. The resemblance to the description of Plato's city of Atlantis as being made out of rings of land and canals made some people believe this island was the right location. The discovery of a fresco believed to be depicting scenes from Atlantis painted on the walls of a building in Santorini heightened the belief. There were also buildings with the distinctive three colour (black, white and red) theme, just as the ancient texts referred to.

However, along with these numerous similarities, there were also many contradictory facts. The dates do not match, for one thing: the destruction of Santorini by a massive volcanic eruption has recently been carbon-dated to have taken place between 1645 BC and 1600 BC. This was certainly the end of the inhabitants of Santorini, but was not the end of the Minoans, who lasted another 200 years in Crete. If the Minoans were the people of Atlantis, their society would have disappeared with the catastrophe, but they did not.

The nature of the disaster was another issue. Plato does not mention a volcanic eruption as the cause of the destruction of Atlantis. The fact that a tsunami followed the eruption on Santorini seems clear, but it is also apparent from the archaeological remains that the destruction was wreaked by the volcanic eruption itself rather than massive flooding. All the buildings are buried in ash and preserved in their original form. If the tsunami had caused the destruction, buildings would have been completely destroyed. Likewise, the general interpretation of Plato's description is that Atlantis sank due to an earthquake and the ensuing tsunami. Following the volcanic eruption and destruction of Santorini, the tsunami destroyed many coastal settlements in Greece and Crete, but it did not wipe out their civilizations.

The natural topography of the island does not match either. Santorini is exceedingly small, and it did not have any of the minerals mined in Atlantis. It certainly did not have any elephants, as Atlantis did. Thus, the description Plato gives of the island of Atlantis does not fit Santorini.

Troy

Other theories have pointed towards Troy, a site located in western Anatolia facing the entrance of the Dardanelles Strait. The theory was based on the fact that the only conflict that coincides with the great battle fought by the Atlanteans was the Battle of Troy. A very valid point, but that was the only similarity. The city of Troy does not even sit on an island, and it never did.

Helike

Some people linked Atlantis to the sunken city of Helike. The fact that we have an actual sunken city that was swallowed by the sea seems to coincide with the myth. The city also worshipped Poseidon as its protector. However, there are major problems with this theory. First, Helike is not an island; it sits on the northern shores of the Peloponnese. But, more importantly, it sank in 373 BC, when Plato would have been alive. Rather than telling this story first-hand, Plato says that Solon was the person who passed on the story of Atlantis and Solon had been dead for nearly 200 years.

A Sunken Island in the Mediterranean

In recent years the possibility that Atlantis lay at the bottom of the sea between Cyprus and Syria has been put forward by Robert Sarmast in his book Discovery of Atlantis. The theory that the island of Atlantis sank following the flooding of the Mediterranean and lay at the bottom of the sea was met with much excitement. But the scientific consensus is that the flooding of the Mediterranean happened many years before any humans existed. Nevertheless, an expedition was organized to look for the ancient city, utilizing bathymetric data of the seabed between Cyprus and Syria. Unfortunately, when they arrived at the proposed site they found only natural formations. Atlantis was not there.

A Sunken Island in the Atlantic Ocean

This theory is still one of the most accepted and oldest candidates. Plato, referring to the Pillars of Heracles, made everyone believe that the island must have been near the Gibraltar strait. But there are major issues with this theory. The Pillars of Heracles never refered to the Gibraltar Strait during the time of Homer or Solon. At the time of Plato there are references of the Pillars referring to various different places around the Mediterranean. The Bosphorus fits the description of the Pillars of Heracles as well as the Gibraltar Strait. Plato said that the strait was facing the land of Gades or Cadiz, but that name was not only used in the south of Spain. In Anatolia, that name, was better known as the river that the Greeks called Hermus and was called Gedir or Cadis by the Lycians. Even Strabo seems to confuse places. Strabo is clearly confused when he places an island called Erytheia near the pillars, as there is no island called 'Erytheia' around Spanish Cadiz nor has there ever been any island there. But there was an 'Erytheia' at the mouth of the Anatolian river, which is now called Chios. The pillars have also been located in Sicily when the tenth Labour of Heracles located Erytheia between Libya and Europe. It seems more likely that the term Pillars of Heracles refered to a narrow passage of water rather than one specific location.

Reference to both the 'Pillars of Heracles' and the 'Atlantic' appear to be ambiguous. Translators have named it as the Atlantic Ocean, but that is not an accurate translation. Plato clearly called it the Atlantic

Sea (Pelagos), not the Atlantic Ocean (Oceanos). The Atlantic Sea being somewhere different than the Atlantic Ocean would explain why Plato mentions that the sea became unnavigable after the disaster. The Atlantic Ocean has always been navigable.

Spain

A recent theory placed the island off the coast of Spain in the area of Cadiz, again based on the belief that the Pillars of Heracles were the Gibraltar Strait. There are some marshlands in the area of modern Cadiz, which led some researchers to believe that this might be the place where the city of Atlantis once stood and that a tsunami may have left it as it appears today. It all seems quite plausible, but again there are flaws. The most obvious is that the location is not an island. Also, there is no evidence of a tsunami or of any ancient city from that period.

The Canary Islands

In 1803, Bory de Saint-Vincent in his 'Essai sur les îles fortunées et l'antique Atlantide' proposed that the Canary Islands, along with Madeira and the Azores, are what remained after Atlantis broke up. But the possibility of the Canary Islands being Atlantis falls apart when you investigate geology and the history of islands. Geologic studies have proven that the islands have been rising steadily for the last few million years and never had any catastrophic subsidence. The Canary Islands had been uninhabited until about 1000 BC, when a group of people called the Guanches occupied the islands. This creates another major problem with the theory: Atlantis was supposed to have flourished a long time before Greek civilization. Since the geology did not match and the archaeological evidence was not there, the Canary Islands was ruled out.

America

When Christopher Columbus discovered America, there were writers who thought that he had discovered Atlantis. They eventually realized, of course, that the land they had found was not even an island and so could not possibly be Atlantis. There were archaeological remains of very early civilizations, but the fact remained that the place was far larger than the island Plato describes.

The Bermuda Triangle

Further afield we have the Bermuda triangle hypothesis. This theory was based on the findings of what has been called the Bimini Road. The place looks like huge slabs placed to form what appears to be a road. Unfortunately, the slabs appear to be a natural formation, and there is no evidence of an advanced civilization here.

Theories relating to the possible location of Atlantis are endless. One suggested that the 'island' was actually in Lake Titicaca, high in the Andes Mountains. A group of pseudo-researchers even claimed that the people of Atlantis were aliens.

Whichever hypothesis you examine; each has certain aspects that carry some validity. Indeed, some present quite reasonable arguments. Still, whatever your views are, none of these theories has managed to convince researchers and academics studying this subject. The fact that when Plato describes the extent of the empire, all his reference locations are known places within the Meditrranean Sea clearly indicates that the mighty empire would have been within that sea.

What Will It Take?

So what would be required to change current perceptions on the existence (or otherwise) of Atlantis and its location and surviving remains?

First of all, it needs to be an island. This would seem to be obvious, but many theoretical locations have been discounted through their failure to conform with the physical description that Plato provided of the island's nature and terrain.

On this island, we should find the ancient harbour town with its circular structure and canals. Plato gives very precise measurements of the rings and canals in the city of Atlantis. There should be evidence of the tsunami that destroyed the city. Debris pushed inland and piled up might be a clue to past devastation. It would be encouraging to find the remains of the temples. The fact that a tsunami hit the city would not explain the complete disappearance of the temples and buildings. Something must be still there. Even better would be finding remains of the boats described. A city with the most advanced harbour in antiquity would have left many sunken or destroyed boats. At least a piece of one of them would be appealing. Finding Poseidon's trident somewhere amid the remains would certainly be the icing on the cake.

Culturally, the island should have been ruled with the same political and religious structures as described in Critias and Timaeus. We should find genetic evidence of how that maritime society spread culture at the dawn of civilization. Its military dominance should also be clear. If there was a city that controlled the seas, there should be some sort of reference to that.

INTRODUCTION

In the next few chapters we will make the case for Cyprus being the island Plato described. Together we will shed some light into the mystery of Atlantis. We will not just find the location of the town of Atlantis, but we will argue in favour of Cyprus being the centre of a major empire that was at the forefront of the development of civilization. I hope to provide enough evidence in order to create a reasonable doubt that history might need to be reconsidered. Together we will rediscover Atlantis, the Cypriot Empire.

ATLATNTIS – THE CYPRIOT EMPIRE

Chapter 1
THE ORIGIN OF CIVILIZATION

The legend of Atlantis is the story of the origins of civilization. This mythical island was believed to be the most technologically, socially and militarily advanced place in the world. It was a place from where, according to Plato's sources, both Greek and Egyptian civilizations were born. Atlantis, without warning, launched an unprecedented attack against the major powers in the region. But, as quickly as it started, it all ended. An earthquake in the Mediterranean Sea gave rise to a tsunami that engulfed the island, washing away one of the world's most influential societies.

In this chapter, we will explore the ways in which ancient Cyprus would have been an ideal spot for the development of a truly advanced civilization, and what evidence we can find for its destruction.

The Bounty of the Land

Around 12,000 years ago, a key development occurred in what we now call the Fertile Crescent. People went through a change that has influenced humanity more than anything else ever since: the introduction of agriculture.

Agriculture required the people to stop being nomads and settle in one place, instantly changing the dynamics of society. With those changes came the appearance of the first towns, the first religious temples, and the first specialization of social roles. Up until then, men had mostly hunted while women had cared for the children and collected fruits and berries. From then on, they developed specialists in agriculture, experts in hunting, builders and so on. Animals were utilized for functions other than for food and hunting. They carried heavy loads and were used to protect crops from pests. The division of roles between people forced them to start trading, and trading led to an abundance of resources. Nearby cultures that lacked resources would try to take them from richer societies. Thus, the need for protective walls around their settlements arose. With that came the need for better weapons to fight the enemy and better tools to increase crop yield. Toolmakers became prized for their skills, and further specialization occurred. The basis for what we call modern society formed. And all this happened in the Fertile Crescent.

Since we know where civilization began, the search for Atlantis should have never left that area. Plato makes it clear that Atlantis was the most highly developed culture of its time, so it is quite logical to assume that the island would have been located near the birthplace of civilization. Cyprus is the only island within the Fertile Crescent. The actual oldest Neolithic Village in the world is actually in Cyprus, just outside Limassol. The site of Klimonas near Agios Tychonas has evidence of an agricultural community as early as 11.100 years ago.

THE ORIGIN OF CIVILIZATION

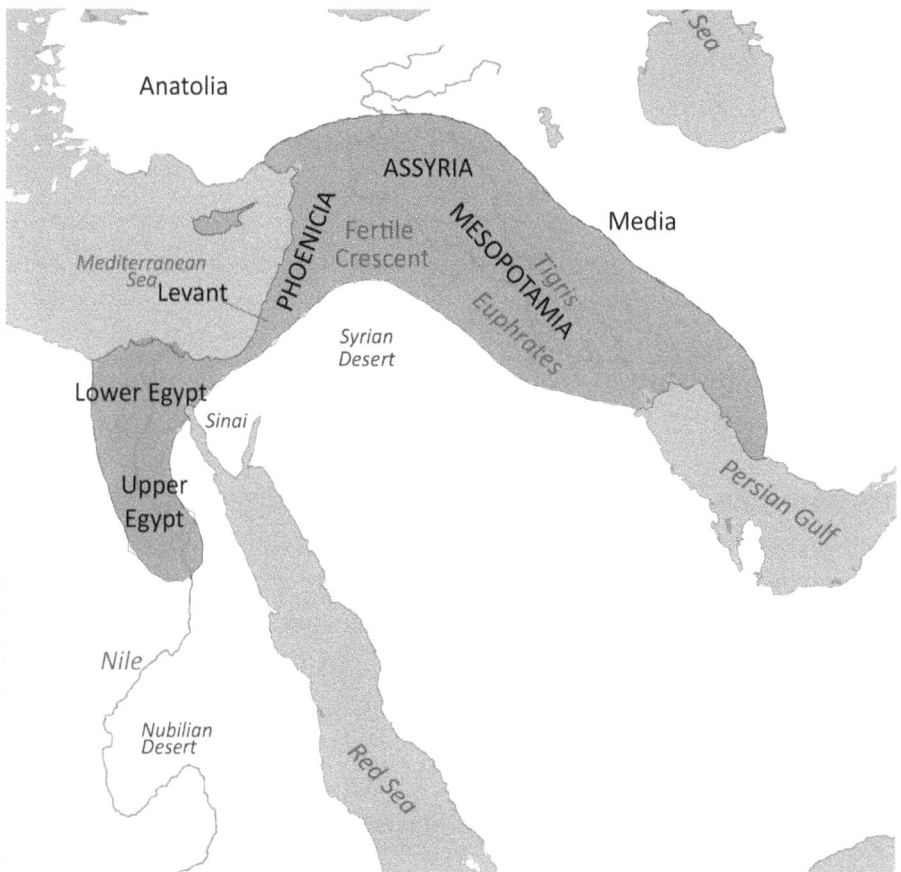

Fig. 1:1: Fertile Crescent Map.[8]

As an advanced society Atlantis must have gone through the Neolithic revolution quite early. Plato speaks in Critias of Atlantis's vast stores of food and drink:

'also the fruit which admits of cultivation, both the dry sort, which is given us for nourishment and any other which we use for food— we call them all by the common name of pulse, and the fruits having a hard rind, affording drinks and meats and ointments, and good store of chestnuts and the like, which furnish pleasure and amusement, and are fruits which spoil with keeping, and the pleasant kinds of dessert, with which we console ourselves after dinner, when we are tired of eating.'

In Cyprus, we know that this type of large-scale agriculture happened very early. Archaeological evidence shows that the first inhabitants of Cyprus had already mastered agriculture as early as 9000 BC. Pulses were farmed from that time and physical evidence has been found in various sites.

Atlantis was also known, according to Critias, to be a sunny, warm place:

'all these that sacred island which then beheld the light of the sun, brought forth fair and wondrous and in infinite abundance.'

This sentence clearly applies to Cyprus, an island that has very sunny and warm weather, made milder by the sea breezes which also temper the winters. Everyone that has tried to grow plants in Cyprus knows that everything grows abundantly there. Agriculture in this land would have been much easier than on the mainland, and thus would have developed much faster.

From Critias, we know that Atlantis's natural abundance directly led to the island's technological development:

'With such blessings the earth freely furnished them; meanwhile they went on constructing their temples and palaces and harbours and docks.'

This seems to be very similar to the situation that Cyprus faced when the first settlers arrived. After living in the harsher terrains of Anatolia or the Middle East they arrived on an island that was extremely fertile. From having to spend the whole time cultivating and hunting in order to make enough to survive, they found themselves in a place where everything grew on its own. Plants seemed not to need any care for them to bear fruit. Animals were so plentiful in a land without natural predators that it did not take the settlers very long to get enough meat to feed the whole community. With that spare time, they were able to devote their energy to other pursuits.

As we've already seen, one of those pursuits was trade. The trade of copper made Cyprus extremely rich. To find a modern-day analogy, consider the Gulf area. Crude oil represents today one of the key products in our civilization, and its control has sparked many conflicts, just like copper used to do in the past. United States, Russia and Saudi Arabia are some of the main producers of oil and, because of that, they have become the richest countries in the modern world. A similar situation could be found in Cyprus in antiquity, where the production of copper gave the island a similar economic advantage. There is only one key difference. Whereas those three countries together produce less than 40% of the oil around the world, Cyprus once supplied 90% of all the copper traded around the Mediterranean. Producing nearly all of the copper during the Bronze Age would have made Cyprus the richest country in the world. In the Nemean ode, Pindar writes:

'For truly, when it is planted with a god's blessing, happiness lasts longer for men; such happiness long ago loaded Kinyras with wealth on sea-washed Cyprus.'[9]

Plato has an even more revealing quote, but this time about Atlantis, in Critias:

'and they had such an amount of wealth as was never before possessed by kings and potentates, and is not likely ever to be again.'

With wealth came not only a life of luxury. We see that technology is always developed in the richest countries. Countries that have funds can spend in developing new technologies. The island would have had the resources to pay for the most advanced research. In cases where other countries had already done the research, Cyprus could just buy the new expertise. It would have been the country with the most advanced technology, just as Plato wrote of Atlantis. But it was not only technology; Social welfare was also way ahead of its time.

Cyprus is known as having the oldest medical insurance in the world. The Idalion Tablet describes an agreement by which doctors would be rewarded by the king for giving free medical treatment to all soldiers injured in battle.

The Most Influential Culture

Atlantis is fabled not just for its wealth and power but also for its influence on other societies. If Atlantis was truly the cultural and economic powerhouse described by Plato, we can expect to see signs of that lasting impact throughout history.

One such example might be language. It is well-known that people from Portugal to India share a common root language that we call Indo-European. This suggests a common origin of the people who actually spoke those languages.

At least three different cultures have preserved the concept of all the people in the known world speaking the same language. The same stories are told in Greek mythology, in the Hebrew Bible, and in a Sumerian text called Enmerkar and the Lord of Aratta. All three texts contain the story of how men started with one language and how confusion arose when the languages multiplied.

The Bible tells the story this way in Genesis 11: 1-9:

> *'Throughout the earth men spoke the same language, with the same vocabulary. Now as they moved eastwards they found a plain in the land of Shinar where they settled. They said to one another, "Come let us make bricks and bake them in the fire." For stone they use bricks, and for mortar they use bitumen...*
> *...Come, let us go down and confuse their language, on the spot so that they can no longer understand one another. The lord*

scattered them thence over the whole face of the earth, and they stopped building the town. It was named Babel therefore, because there the Lord confused the language of the whole earth...'

A very similar myth is told about Phoroneus and Hermes in Greco-Roman mythology by Hyginus in Fabula 143:

'Inachus, son of Oceanus, begat Phoroneus by his sister Argia, and he is said to have been the first of mortals to rule. Men for many centuries before lived without town or laws, speaking one tongue under the rule of Jove. But after Mercury had explained the languages of men then discord arose among mortals, which was not pleasing to Jove. And so he gave over the first rule to Phoroneus, because he was first to make offerings to Juno.'

The Romans attributed the origin of the confusion to Mercury, who was their version of the Greek god Hermes. Hermes would try to fix the confusion by becoming the interpreter; ever since, in Greek, the role of the interpreter has been called 'Ermenautes'.

The language that was the origin of all those languages is called Proto-Indo-European. Many attempts have been made to trace the origin of that common language. The oldest attempt was recorded by Herodotus in the 5th century BC, writing about a Pharaoh of around the 7th century BC:

'Now before Psammetichus became king of Egypt, the Egyptians believed that they were the oldest people on earth. But ever since Psammetichus became king and wished to find out which people were the oldest, they have believed that the Phrygians were older than they, and they than everybody else.

Psammetichus, when he was in no way able to learn by inquiry which people had first come into being, devised a plan by which he took two new-born children of the common people and gave them to a shepherd to bring up among his flocks. He gave instructions that no one was to speak a word in their hearing; they were to stay by themselves in a lonely hut, and in due time the shepherd was to bring goats and give the children their milk and do everything else necessary.

Psammetichus did this, and gave these instructions, because he wanted to hear what speech would first come from the children, when they were past the age of indistinct babbling. And he had his wish; for one day, when the shepherd had done as he was told for two years, both children ran to him stretching out their hands and calling "Bekos!" as he opened the door and entered.

When he first heard this, he kept quiet about it; but when, coming often and paying careful attention, he kept hearing this same word, he told his master at last and brought the children into the king's presence as required. Psammetichus then heard them himself, and asked to what language the word "Bekos" belonged; he found it to be a Phrygian word, signifying bread. Reasoning from this, the Egyptians acknowledged that the Phrygians [a people believed to be from central Anatolia] were older than they."[10]

Many more attempts have been made since then. In the 16th century, European visitors to the Indian subcontinent began to suggest similarities between Indo-Aryan, Iranian and European languages, but it was not until Franz Bopp's Comparative Grammar, which appeared between 1833 and 1852, that Indo-European studies became an academic discipline.

Until recently, one of the most widely accepted theories was that the originators of the Indo-European language appeared during the copper age in the Dnieper Volga area. This theory, the Kurgan hypothesis, placed the origin of the European languages in 4000 BC. But all that is changing. Some linguists now believe that the languages must have developed far earlier. Archaeologist and paleolinguist Colin

Renfrew suggested that the movements of the languages would have followed the same routes as the spread of agriculture. Renfrew and many others place the origin of the Indo-European language in the Anatolia region, just as Herodotus did.

One of the most conclusive research studies on the subject was conducted by a group of linguists, statisticians, and virologists from the KU Leuven University in Belgium.[11] They examined the evolution of the languages and viruses, noting that viruses and language family trees were very similar. The difference is that viruses have a much more precise and less erratic family tree. They then compared the data of all the languages that overlapped with the arrival of certain viruses in that area. From there, they managed to locate and date the origin of all Indo-European languages somewhere between 8,000 and 9,000 years ago in southern Anatolia.

Another study was carried out by John Moores University in Liverpool. A team of anthropologists analysed the remains of 63 human skeletons from 7700 to 6650 BC in three archaeological sites in the Middle East: Tell Halula near Aleppo, Tell Ramad on Mount Hermon, and Tell Dja'de El Mughara in northern Syria. They compared DNA samples from the skeletons to those from sites in Europe to find out when these genetic markers first appear in various European locations.

The results of this study changed the views they had of a Europe settled from Eurasia. The results point towards a migration that started around 9000 BC with the arrival of the first settlers to Cyprus. From Cyprus the colonization continued by sea towards Crete, a move that happened around 7000 BC. They arrived on the Greek mainland towards 6600 BC and, by 6000 BC, they started to move west. They reached the coast of the Iberian Peninsula, in the area of Catalonia, by 5800 BC and to the area of Lisbon at around 5400 BC. They did not reach the inland areas until 5200 BC, proving that they first colonized the coastal littorals and then moved inland as the population expanded. In Eastern Europe the migration followed the route of the Danube. This was the first confirmation that the Neolithic revolution spread by sea or rivers from the Middle East into Europe by 6000 BC.

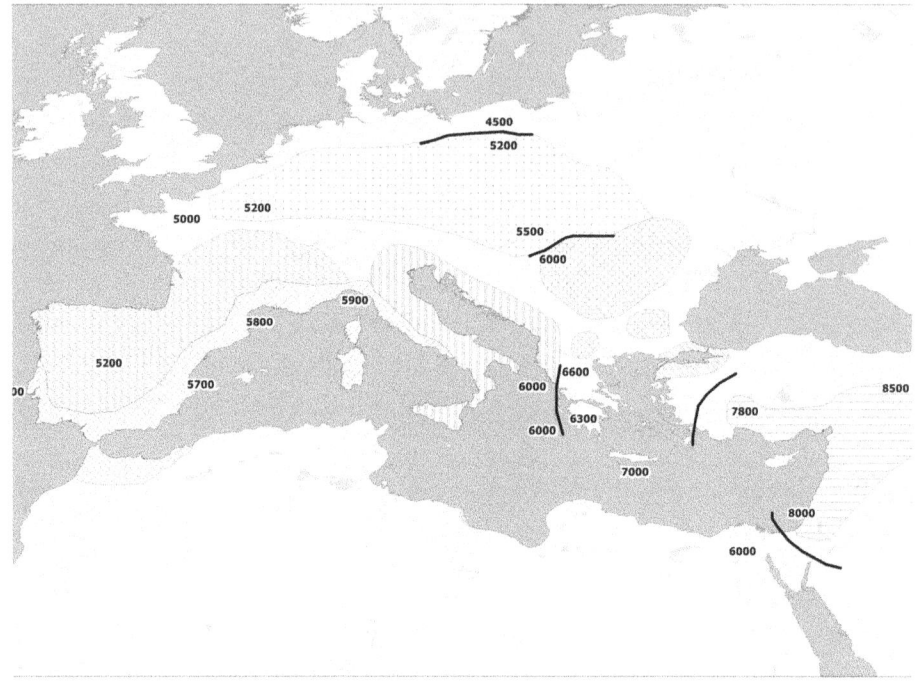

Fig. 1.2: Map of the spread of Neolithic farming cultures in Europe.[12]

But it also points towards a much greater role for Cyprus in the development of Europe. A migration made by sea clearly by a seafaring society. Once researchers had analysed the data, they produced a map to show the actual variance from the original markers and how long it would take for the rest of Anatolia, the Aegean, Arabia, Egypt and the Afghanistan-Pakistan area to include those genetic markers. This map indicates that Cyprus was at the centre of the development of all civilizations from Europe, North Africa and Asia. Cyprus was ground zero for the Neolithic expansion.

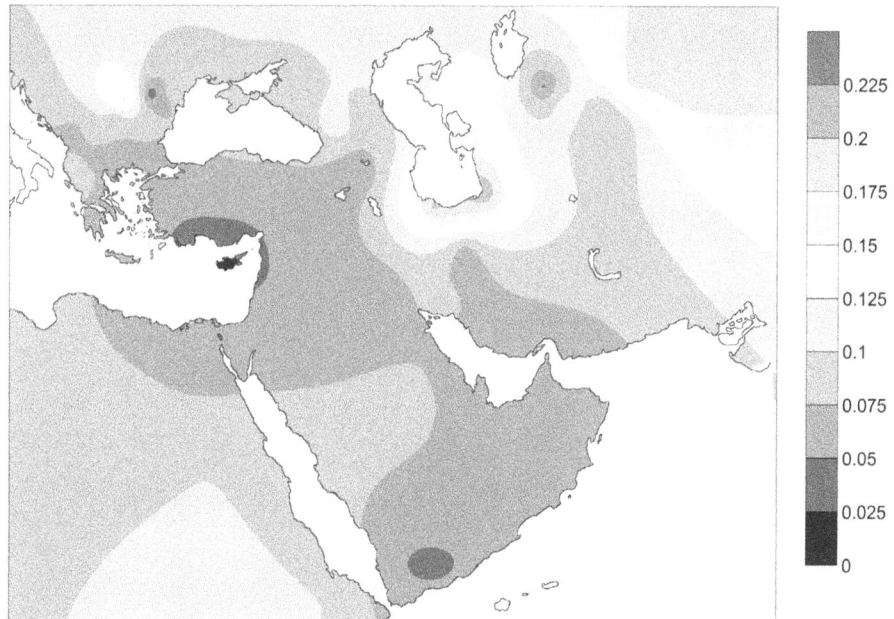

Fig. 1.3: Contour map of Fst distances between the PPNB population and modern populations of the database.[13]

If the migrations follow one direction, why do we think that writing originated in Mesopotamia with cuneiform? The answer is that it did not. In the area where we will locate the Empire of Atlantis, we find examples of writing at least 2,000 years older than cuneiform.

The most notable is the Dispilio tablet. It was found very near the village of Dispilio next to the Orestias Lake during the July 1993 excavation campaign. The tablet, made out of cedar wood, has ten rows of symbols. Peculiarly, Cedar was not a local wood, but one readily available in Cyprus. Once carbon-dated, it was established that the tablet was from 5200 BC. The signs are not arbitrary, as in the Danube area similar symbols have been found in what has been called the Vinča culture. Dating also to the 6–5 millennium BC they have very similar signs.

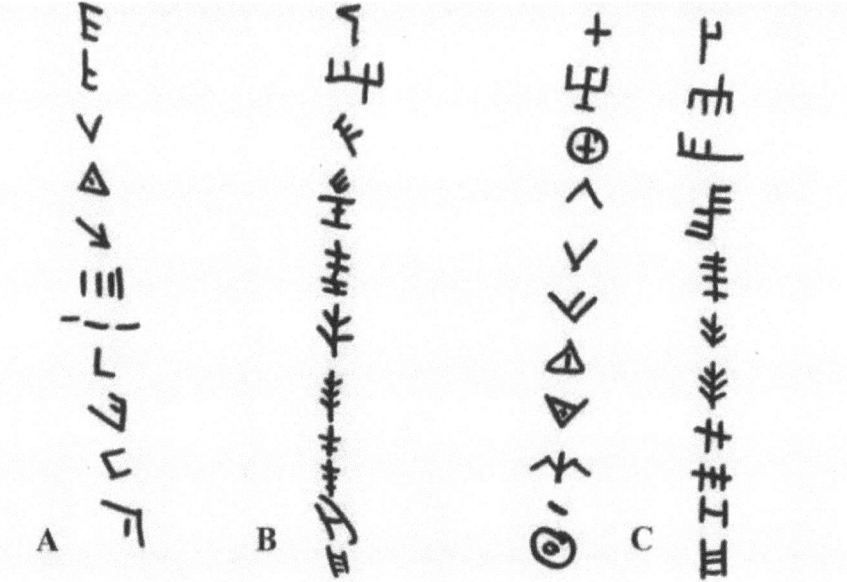

Figure 6 (A): Samples of carved "signs" on the wooden tablet and other clay finds from Dispilio; (B) samples of Linear A signs; (C) samples of signs on Paleoeuropean clay tablets (modified from Hourmouziadis 1996).

Fig. 1.4: Dispilio tablet signs compared to Linear A[14]

These symbols and script appear at the time of the first westward migrations and it would be very difficult to believe that the script would have followed a different path from that of the development of the Neolithic. It is therefore reasonable to suggest that the script would, slowly, also have followed the same path as that of agriculture (as shown in the DNA map) and therefore to have originated in Cyprus.

When agriculture, wealth, language, and other cultural developments all originated from a single area, that area must have had tremendous importance to the ancient world. All this would indicate that Cyprus could certainly be the sociocultural epicentre that Plato was describing when he spoke about Atlantis.

The Ten Kingdoms of Atlantis

'Each of the ten kings in his own division and in his own city had the absolute control of the citizens.'
(Plato, Critias)

We can see that the political system of Atlantis was a confederation of city kingdoms. Power was believed to have been given to the kings by the gods, and the kings were regarded as their direct descendants. The gods divided the world into ten parts and gave them to one of their descendants to rule the land. In each of the ten kingdoms, the king had total control of his own people, where he ruled as he pleased and administered justice as he saw fit, as long as his decisions did not affect any of the other kingdoms.

This system of government is probably the most striking similarity between Atlantis and Cyprus. Cyprus was also divided into ten city kingdoms, which seem to have lived in harmony with each other up until the end of the Bronze Age.

Very little historical information is available regarding these kingdoms. The most reliable evidence dates from the years 673–672 BC, where there is a record of the ten kingdoms of Cyprus paying tribute to the Assyrian king Esarhaddon.

Located in the British Museum, the Prism of Esarhaddon names; Ekistura, king of Idalion; Pilagura, king of Chytrus; Kisu, king of Soli; Ituandar, king of Paphos; Erisu, king of Silli; Damasu, king of Curium; Atmesu, king of Tamesi; Darmisi, king of Karti-hadasti; Unasagusu, king of Ledra; Bususu of Nuria. Ten kings of Iatnana.[15]

The Cypriot kingdoms have been identified as Idalion, Chytroi, Salamis, Paphos, Soloi, Kourion, Tamassos, Ledra, (the 'new city' traditionally identified as Kition) and Noure (possibly Amathous).[16] The Roman geographer Strabo wrote that:

'The Cypriots were first ruled in their several cities by kings, but since the Ptolemaic kings became lords over Egypt, Cyprus too passed to them.'[17]

Having ten kingdoms created a very confusing situation with regard to the naming of the island. Today we know the island as Cyprus, which is believed to have originated from either the name of the goddess Kypris, the metal found all over the island (cupprum), or the henna plant that used to be called kypros. But the fact is that this little island had more names than any other place on the planet. Akamantis, Iera Nissos, Aspelia, Kition, Khettim, Makaria, Eveleos, Kryptos, Khethima, Kyoforos, Alassia, Kerastis, Amathousia, Sfikia, Miionis, Kolinia, Aeria, Tharsis, Nea Ioustiniana—these are only a few of the known names used when talking about the island. Most written sources reference the individual kingdoms on the island, rather than the island as a whole. Other names commonly used are epithets of the island. Makaria has been translated as 'Happy' or 'Blessed'. Eveleos relates to the olive trees and oil. The number and variety of names appear endless. Naming the whole island from the name of the one city was very common in Cyprus. Giving the name of the city of Atlantis to the whole island would not have been unusual at the time of Plato.

The Cypriot system of kingdoms based on cities would many years later be the foundation of Greek society. City-states would appear in Greece right at the time that the Assyrians seized control of the Cypriot city-states. It is not a coincidence that some historians call that period of Greek culture the Orientalizing period.

The ten kingdoms of Cyprus were ruled by kings, acting as the head priests of the superior gods that gave them power. The best evidence for this comes from Paphos, where the king had to perform some rituals at the temple in order to establish and maintain sovereignty. This seems to be exactly the same arrangement as Plato describes in Atlantis, with kings that had their power validated by the gods. Rule in Atlantis was certainly not dictatorial, as these priestly kings are described as:

'laying hold of the souls by persuasion.'

Furthermore,

'There were many special laws affecting the several kings inscribed about the temples, but the most important was the following: They were not to take up arms against one another, and they were all to come to the rescue if any one in any of their cities attempted to overthrow the royal house; like their ancestors, they were to deliberate in common about war and other matters, giving the supremacy to the descendants of Atlas. And the king was not to have the power of life and death over any of his kinsmen unless he had the assent of the majority of the ten.'
(Plato, Critias)

Thus, in Atlantis, the kings had to follow certain laws, which was something unheard of in ancient times. Kings were supposed to be supreme rulers; the Egyptian pharaohs, the kings of Babylon, and the Hittite rulers never had to follow any written rules. In Atlantis, the laws were written on a column made of orichalcum and on the temple walls, available for everyone to see. Not until the signing of the Magna Carta by King John more than 2,000 years later would another king publicly submit to the rule of law.

The political arrangements of the island seem so advanced for its time that it is difficult to comprehend. A political system that operated by 'laying hold of the souls by persuasion' can only function if the people so persuaded agree on the acts to follow. That can only be achieved if there is a process to determine the will of the people. That process forms the basis of democracy.

The Seeds of Democracy

Democracy is believed to have started in Greece in the 5th century BC, and one of the most vocal advocates for the changes that led to that political system was a man named Solon.

Solon (638–558 BC) was one of the most revered people in ancient Greece. He did a lot of travelling, mainly between Athens, Lycia, Cyprus and Egypt. After he had established his democratic reforms in Athens, he was believed to have travelled for ten years, so that the Athenians could not induce him to repeal any of his laws. His first stop was Egypt. There, according to Herodotus, he visited the Pharaoh Amasis II. According to Plutarch, he also discussed philosophy with two Egyptian priests, Psenophis of Heliopolis and Sonchis of Sais. According to Plato's dialogues Timaeus and Critias, he visited Neith's temple at Sais and received from the priests there an account of the history of Atlantis. Next Solon sailed to Cyprus and, according to tradition, he oversaw the construction of a new capital for a local king, in gratitude for which the king named it Soloi.

Solon's travels finally brought him to Sardis, capital of Lydia. According to Herodotus and Plutarch, Solon met Croesus and gave the Lydian king advice, which Croesus failed to appreciate until it was too late. Croesus had considered himself to be the happiest man alive, so Solon had advised him: 'Count no man happy until he be dead.' At any minute, Solon warned, fortune might turn on even the happiest man and make his life miserable. It was only after he had lost his kingdom to the Persian king Cyrus, while awaiting execution, that

Croesus acknowledged the wisdom of Solon's advice.

After his return to Athens, Solon became a staunch opponent of Pisistratus, who attempted to roll back Solon's democratic reforms. In protest, and as an example to others, Solon stood outside his own home in full armour, urging all who passed to resist the machinations of the would-be tyrant. But his efforts were in vain. Solon died shortly after Pisistratus usurped by force the autocratic power that Athens had once freely bestowed upon him. According to one account, Solon died in Cyprus and, in accordance with his will, his ashes were scattered around Salamis, the Greek island where he was supposedly born.

This is how history remembered him, but there is a minor issue with this version of the story. Solon could not have been able to oversee the construction of Soloi, since Soloi had already existed for at least 100 years. The Sargon Stele from the 7th century BC mentions the ten kingdoms of Cyprus, including Soloi. The Assyrian king Esarhaddon (680–669 BC) later mentions Soloi as one of the kingdoms of Cyprus. Solon was not born until at least 638 BC. A s it turns out, 'Solon' is more likely a term for what you would call someone from Soloi. Etymologically, it makes much more sense that Solon was named after Soloi than Soloi being named after Solon. If the city was named after Solon, it should have been called Solona. The fact that Solon actually built a city in the kingdom of Soloi is not in doubt, as a new city appeared on the western coast at that time. The new city was also called Soloi, its name derived from the previous city, and not from the city planner.

This goes against the popular understanding that Solon was an Athenian from birth. The fact that most accounts were written as late as 100 AD, more than 600 years after the time of Solon, must have added to the misunderstanding. However, the idea that Solon's name derived from the town and not the other way round was argued by Eustathios of Thessaloniki, who wrote just before the Third Crusade: 'But how "solecism" is a synthesis of this "Solos" or "Soloi" is found in the writings of Periegetes. It seems that the lawgiver Solon also derives his name hence.'[18]

The idea that Solon was from the island of Salamis in Greece was questioned much earlier though. Plutarch wrote in Lives: 'The story that his ashes were scattered about the island Salamis is too strange to be easily believed, or be thought anything but a mere fable.'[19]

If Solon was from Soloi, all the history related to him becomes more understandable. It makes sense that a man from Soloi would recommend some changes to improve the lives of the Athenians. These changes he would have already seen working in his native land. That he was a highly regarded person in Cyprus is obvious, since the king of Soloi gave him the freedom to design a city. It would also make sense that he would warn Croesus about the impending Persian invasion that the Cypriots had already suffered.

The high status he held in his original country is what made the Athenians respect him. Once he introduced his reforms in Athens, following Cyprus as a model, he then left to go back home.

Cyprus being more closely connected geographically to the people of Lycia and Lydia would also explain why the Greeks credited to Solon the introduction of a Lydian invention: coinage. The first gold coins from Lydia would not be circulated in Greece for some years after Solon, but the fact that he would have passed through Lydia to get to Athens from Cyprus would explain that connection. After all, how would he have known of the coins and the Cypriot political and economic systems if, as legend tells us, he did all of his travelling after making the reforms? Moreover, Solon's reforms encouraged foreign trade, particularly maritime trade. At the time, the Greeks did not have a merchant navy, and sea trade was dominated by the Cypriots and the Phoenicians. It seems that when Solon was encouraging the

Greeks to develop their own maritime trade, he had some familiarity as to the potential benefits.

Ancient writers say that Solon spent his old age on the island of Cyprus and that he died there. Would it not be more reasonable to assume that he was buried in the city of Salamis in Cyprus rather than taken to the island of Salamis in Greece, with all the logistic issues that this would imply? The island of Salamis was something of a backwater during Solon's time. For Salamis Island to be the last resting place for such an illustrious individual, famed throughout the ancient world, seems unlikely. In fact, nearly everything attributed to Solon's Salamis seems not to have existed on Salamis Island during this period. There are records of a ruler of Salamis, but not a single inscription has ever been found on the island. A famous theatre festival was supposed to have taken place there, but no theatre has ever been discovered. The Cypriot city of Salamis, however, had both a ruler and a theatre. When ancient writers wrote of the 'island' of Salamis they were perhaps referring to the island where the city of Salamis was located, in much the same way as they often referred to Cyprus by its various constituent kingdoms.

Over the centuries, some Cypriots have tried to reclaim Solon from the Greeks. In 1788 Archimandrita Kyprianou, father of Cypriot modern history, wrote:

'About the year 3398 Solon (602BC), one of the famed seven sages (wise men) of Greece during this time, arrived in Athens. Born in Salamis of Cyprus, he was invited at that time by the Athenians while he was staying with Croesus, king of the Lydians in Asia Minor. The Athenians needed Solon to put things in Athens in order and to help moderate the cruel legislation imposed by Dracon, the previous governor of the Athenians.

While in Athens this great man, and hearing that his special Motherland (Cyprus) was tortured and suffering hardships from the

Megareans, and at such a degree that they have to promise that they would accept to pay tribute to them. Nevertheless, the sea pirates of Megara, perhaps exploiting the lack of unity among the Cypriots as well as their enmities, they insisted for more.
Solon sought and maintained the favour of the Athenians and as he was granted enough military assistance, came to Cyprus and after chasing out the Megareans, brought peace among the Kings and put everything in order in the Island.'[20]

Solon was not only Cypriot but also played a crucial role in shaping the story of Atlantis by confirming Plato's story. If Solon knew so well the island of Cyprus, can we then recognize his homeland in the story of Atlantis?

Chapter 2
ATLANTEAN GEOGRAPHY

We know that Plato's description of Atlantis is incomplete, but the few pages that we have are full of information that should enable us to identify the island. If we slowly analyse Plato's writings, it should be easy to see that there is no other place on the planet but Cyprus that had everything that Plato says Atlantis had. So, let's see how Cyprus and Atlantis compare.

Of all the factors regarding the identity of Atlantis, two always seem to recur with every new theory. One is the size of the island and the other is the timeframe Plato uses. In order to locate the island successfully, they need to be addressed.

The size of the island has always been hotly debated. As it was the most common unit of distance of the time, Plato uses stadia as the standard measurement unit for his whole text. He measures the distance from the Acropolis to the sea with stadia. He measures the size of the city with stadia. He even uses squared stadia to measure areas.

In modern translations of Plato's texts, the island of Atlantis is as big as Libya and Asia. Combining the sizes of what the ancients used to call Libya and Asia, we find that the island would not fit inside the Mediterranean Sea. Indeed, it would hardly fit in the Atlantic Ocean. So, why would Plato use for one of the most vital measurements of the island, anything but stadia? Why would he make the size of the island so imprecise?

The answer is that probably he did not. In 1969, J.V. Luce wrote that it all came from an incorrect translation of the ancient Greek language. Where the earliest translators interpreted 'mezon' as 'larger than', they should have translated the words instead as 'meson' or 'in between'.[21] Therefore, it is reasonable to deduce that Plato actually meant the island of Atlantis was located between, rather than bigger than Libya and Asia.

In that context, it makes more sense that he used stadia for size and distances and two points of reference to pinpoint the location. Using this more precise location narrows down the candidates for the lost island. If you draw lines from ancient Libya towards what they called Asia, one island seems to be right in the middle: the island of Cyprus. Another big point of contention is the date Plato gives. Was there a society in 9500 BC as technologically advanced as he describes?

We know that around that time there were some advanced societies able to build places like Göbekli Tepe. But what could not have happened is the war Plato describes, pitting Atlantis against Europe and Asia, where Athens supposedly took the upper hand. This war was supposed to have been fought using triremes, a kind of boat that certainly did not exist in 9500 BC. In the texts of Plato, the people of Atlantis had metallurgy skills that would not be mastered for another 5,000 years. But there are many other faults in the myth. Athens, a key player in the battle, did not even exist then. The first signs of human settlement in Athens are from the Acropolis, which date to around 2,000 years later. It seems clear that the date of the war mentioned in the story of Atlantis could not have been as given by Plato.

But the date is not a mistake, nor is it a coincidence. Nine thousand years before Plato's time is exactly when Cyprus was first inhabited. Cyprus is also the only island in the world that, at that time, was inhabited by a Neolithic society. This makes Cyprus the only realistic candidate of advanced island society from around 9500 BC.

So when was the war fought? Anyone who knows the period of the end of the Bronze Age will recognize the events described by Plato. Plato writes in Timaeus about the mighty power of Atlantis, a society that ruled the seas:

'For these histories tell of a mighty power which unprovoked made an expedition against the whole of Europe and Asia.'

Any historian would tell you that this is exactly what seems to have happened during that period, when what the Egyptians called the 'Sea People' destroyed most of Greece, Anatolia, Syria and the area of today's Israel. This Sea People also took on the Egyptians, who avoided annihilation but would never recover to be the strong empire they once were.

What the ancient Egyptians called the Sea People, a society that launched an unprovoked attack and then, overnight, disappeared, seems to be exactly the same that Plato believed through his sources. The war that the Sea People started was the war that geoarchaeologist Eberhard Zangger has described as World War 0, a war that ended the Bronze Age and ushered in the Iron Age.

A society capable of wiping out the most powerful forces in the region must have had a massive army. And to have a massive army, it must have had a vast territory where it would have lived. In short, and as Plato says in Timaeus it had, it would have needed an empire:

'Now in this island of Atlantis there was a great and wonderful empire which had rule over the whole island and several others,

and over parts of the continent, and, furthermore, the men of Atlantis had subjected the parts of Libya within the columns of Heracles as far as Egypt, and of Europe as far as Tyrrhenia.'

The Empire of Atlantis must have been 'within' the Mediterranean basin 'the Pillars of Heracles', as he calls it, and not beyond. The island of Cyprus would have been the centre of the empire. The several islands mentioned must be the Greek Islands; after all, they were supposed to control the seas.

The idea that all the islands were under the control of Cyprus should not be such a surprise. The Hebrews had a common name for all the islands of the Aegean: the islands of Kittim. The term clearly preserved the idea of the town they called Kittim (Kition) as the centre of rule of all the Aegean. As Theodoret of Cyrrhus wrote in the 5th century AD:

'Kittion is a city in Cyprus and known by that name to the present day. The aspiration (of the k), in the Hebrew language, shows the relationship with Chettieim. Cyprus was at that time ruling the islands; therefore he calls the Greek islands Chettieim.'[22]

The area mentioned by Plato as 'over parts of the continent' should not be difficult to find either. We know, more or less, that most of inland Anatolia and the Middle East were under the control of the Hittites and Egyptians at the time. It is therefore impossible that the 'parts of the continent' would have been there. Only the coastal area of the Middle East that would later be called Phoenicia was spared from the general devastation during the Bronze Age collapse, making this area a very likely candidate.

What was called Lycia was probably also part of the empire of the 'Sea People'. In a letter to the Egyptian pharoah, the king of Alashiya refers to the men of Lukki (Lycia) attacking them and being the same that attacked Egypt.

The area of western Anatolia could also have been part of the empire, but that area was in dispute with the Hittites. It seems that the alliance of Alaksandu of Wilusa with the Hittites was what really triggered the start of the war. Wilusa, the Hittite name for Troy, is also mentioned in a Hittite letter dated to the period as the town that they were fighting for. The name Alaksandu of Wilusa most historians equate to Paris of Troy, whom the Greeks called Alexander.

Another area of the empire was probably in North Africa, since Plato says in Timaeus that:

'the men of Atlantis had subjected the parts of Libya within the columns of Heracles as far as Egypt.'

Since we know that in antiquity the term Libya referred to the whole of northern Africa, it seems clear that the whole of the coast of northern Africa would have been part of that empire. This seems to be confirmed by the fact that some of the ethnic groups that attacked Egypt came from Libya and were called Libu by the Egyptians.

On the northern end of the Mediterranean Sea the empire stretched as far as Tyrrhenia, according to Plato. Tyrrhenia being west of Italy implies that all the lands in coastal Europe all the way to Italy were under control of the people of Atlantis.

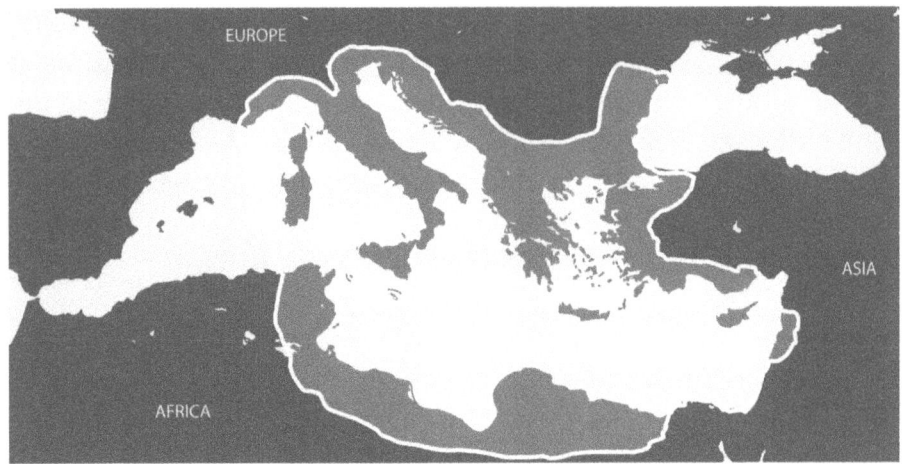

Fig. 2.1: Extent of the Atlantean Empire[23]

These broad borders seem to match the land that Hebrew sources called the isles of Kittim. Josephus wrote:

'the name Chethim given by the Hebrews to all islands and the most maritime countries.'[24]

This resembles remarkably Plato's words in Timaeus:

'had rule over the whole island and several others, and over parts of the continent.'

If Cyprus was the centre of a vast Mediterranean Empire, that would match both the Egyptian description of a conquering Sea People and Plato's description of the advanced society based in Atlantis. The next step is to see if the other descriptions of the island match.

Trade

One of the first things that Plato mentions in Critias is that Atlantis was a major trader in antiquity:

'For because of the greatness of their empire many things were brought to them from foreign countries.'

Cyprus was a major trading point during the Bronze Age between Egypt, Middle East, Mesopotamia and the Aegean. The only two Bronze Age boats found in the Mediterranean suggest that trade was carried out using Cypriot ships that had Cypriot captains with large amounts of Cypriot products. Evidence of the trade is apparent in the many Cypriot items found in places like Babylon or Egypt and foreign items found in Cyprus which are on display in the Cyprus Museum in Nicosia. But not just trade; presents sent from foreign lands appear in the correspondence found in the Amarna tablets in Egypt—gifts sent to and from Cyprus just to maintain good relations with their neighbours.

Precious Metals

A variety of metals were supposedly mined from Atlantis, according to Critias:

'In the first place, they dug out of the earth whatever was to be found there, solid as well as fusile, and that which is now only a name and was then something more than a name, orichalcum, was dug out of the earth in many parts of the island, being more precious in those days than anything except gold.'

It is well known that Cyprus was once the biggest producer of copper. The island's name is believed to relate to the ancient word for copper (cupprum). Either the name of the island was derived from the name of the mineral or the mineral was given the name of the island as recognition of its source.

Copper mines in Cyprus are mainly found around the slopes of the Troodos Mountains. One of the main areas of extraction of copper was in the northwest coast around the area of the ancient kingdom of Soloi, 8 kilometres inland from Morphou Bay. There we find a mine that has been active since 4000 BC. There are also ancient copper mines in the area of Khirokitia and Kalavasos, as well as in the area between the Troodos Mountain and Kition and Stavrovouni. But what is not so well known is that Cyprus also had silver and gold mines. Minerals that have been extracted from these same copper mines indicate that deposits of silver and gold would have also been known in the Bronze Age. These mines continued to produce gold and silver up to the end of the 20th century.

Where copper was first discovered has not been proven, but we know that it happened at around 9000 BC. During the Roman era, Pliny the Elder believed it happened in Cyprus.[25] In his Natural History, Pliny the Elder says that the Cypriot king Kinyras was the first to discover copper mines. Since then up until Roman times, more than 200,000 tons of pure copper would have been mined in Cyprus. Big furnaces had to be fired in order to extract the metal. That caused a major environmental problem. Most Cypriot forests were cut down in order to get the wood to keep the furnaces going.

Copper was so abundant in Cyprus that people believed that you could plant it. Aristotle wrote in Mirabilia:

'They also say that in Cyprus in the district called Tyrrias bronze behaves in a similar way. For apparently they cut it into small pieces and sow it; then when the rain comes it grows, and puts out shoots and so is collected.'[26]

Copper made Cyprus a major trading hub. Everyone required copper to produce tools and these same traders wanted Cypriot copper. Soon, they understood that by mixing the copper with tin, you could create a much stronger product. At around 2500 BC the Cypriot Bronze Age had started. With copper and especially with bronze a major step forward occurred in weapon-making. Man progressed from stone axes to metal spears, arrows and swords. With these more durable weapons, large armies started to develop and specialise.

Orichalcum

Another mineral mentioned by Plato in Critias is orichalcum:

> *'that which is now only a name and was then something more than a name, orichalcum, was dug out of the earth in many parts of the island.'*

Scientists still do not agree on the exact composition of this mysterious mineral. From the nature of the word we can deduce that it might have been a copper alloy, as chalcum is the ancient Greek word for copper. The mineral is also mentioned as being used in the construction of another of the most searched temples in antiquity: the biblical Temple of Solomon.

The Romans believed that orichalcum was an alloy made out of gold and copper. They presumed the name came from aurum, gold in Latin, and chalcum. That would certainly fit the description, since it was said that the metal shone like gold. However, this translation is definitely wrong. The word likely came from a combination of oros, which means mountain in Greek, and chalcum: the 'copper of the mountains'.

The most likely candidate for this legendary substance is brass. Made out of a combination of copper and zinc, brass was often used as a gold substitute because of its shiny 'golden' appearance. In the mines at the foothills of the Troodos Mountains there are still zinc residues to be found. Therefore, a natural combination of the two minerals in the same mines does not seem so far-fetched.

Whatever it was, it must have been very scarce, since by the time of the Romans it was no longer available. Pliny records:

'In Cyprus,... and specially gold-copper (Orichalcum), which for a long time now has not been found, the ground being exhausted.'[27]

The true nature of orichalcum may have been lost to history if not for a recent discovery. In 2014 a group of divers found a shipwreck that sunk about 2,600 years ago off the southern coast of Sicily. In the wreck they found 39 ingots of copper and zinc alloy. The ingots were about 75-80 percent copper and 15-20 percent zinc, with small percentages of nickel, lead and iron. This seem to coincide with the description of the then mythical metal. The provenance of the ship is not known, but they believed it came from the east.

There are not many ancient records of producers of mountain-copper around the world, but the few that exist generally point to Cyprus. In an Akkadian document from Mari and Babylonia from before 1797 BC there is a reference that was translated as:

'4 talents, 50 minas (145kg) of mountain-copper; 50 minas mountain-copper from Alashiya.'[28]

This is the clearest reference to the famous mountain-copper and its origin. Alashiya, an ancient name for Cyprus, is called out as the place where you can find this elusive metal otherwise identified with Atlantis. In the Homeric Hymn to Aphrodite VI we have an account of Aphrodite jewlery being made out of Orichalcum.

'On her inmortal head they laid a crown of gold that was wonderfully made and in the pierced lobes of her ears they hung flowers of copper from the mountains (Orichalcum) and precious gold.'[29]

There is no doubt that Orichalcum was available in Cyprus and Atlantis.

Wood

According to Plato's Critias, Atlantis was also heavily wooded:

'There was an abundance of wood for carpenter's work.'

When you think of the island of Cyprus today you do not think of luscious forests, but that was what the island looked like at the time of Plato's writing. Continuous man-made deforestation has plagued the island for centuries, due mainly to the large amount of wood that was needed for building and to smelt metals from the copper mines. The most precious wood in ancient times was the cedar tree (Cedrus libani). The Egyptians used cedar wood in elite buildings and the pharaoh's ships. It was also the preferred wood to construct temples, including the Temple of Solomon. More commonly associated with Lebanon, cedars were in ancient times widely spread around the Troodos Mountains, where a few can still be found. Though very similar to the Lebanese cedar, the Cyprus cedar is now classified as a separate species (Cedrus brevifolia). During the time of Pliny, the largest cedars were the Cypriot species, as Pliny noted in Natural History:

'The largest cedar is reported to have been grown in Cyprus and to have been felled to make a mast for a galley.'

Oak was another very valuable tree that Cyprus used to have in abundance but is quite rare today. The variety that grows in Cyprus (Quercus alnifolia or Golden Oak) is endemic to Cyprus. It was so much appreciated that is still the national tree of Cyprus.

There is also the Cyprus tree, or Cypress tree, a tree sacred to both Apollo and Artemis that probably gets its name from its abundance on the island. The Cyprus tree was, though, more of a daily use timber than the more 'holy' cedar. Beams of houses were made out of Cyprus trees until very recently. Ancient weapons were probably also made out of Cyprus trees, since its strong and straight wood makes it ideal for use in spears.

Cyprus was also replete with fruit trees, such as pistachio, olive, myrtle, carob and pomegranate. The desertification created by the overexploitation of all these trees has given Cyprus its modern more barren appearance, but there is substantial evidence that during the Bronze Age Cyprus resembled a subtropical forest. Therefore, the volume and diversity of trees that Cyprus had back then also matches perfectly descriptions of Atlantis.

Animals

With regard to the species of animals, Plato writes in Critias that Atlantis was home to:

'sufficient maintenance for tame and wild animals. Moreover, there were a great number of elephants in the island.'

The first people that arrived on the island of Cyprus must have come by boat making them the first known seafaring society. By this means they also introduced many animals that would multiply prodigiously in Cyprus. Pigs, cows, goats, cats, and many other animals arrived in the same boats as the first inhabitants of Cyprus.

Elephants arrived in Cyprus during the Pleistocene era, well before the arrival of humans. Over many years of living on the island, Cypriot elephants gradually reduced their size, eventually becoming a sub-species called the Cyprus dwarf. Remains of the Cyprus dwarf elephant were first discovered in the Kyrenia area in 1902 and subsequently uncovered on the Akrotiri peninsula in southern Cyprus. From the remains found in the Akrotiri site, it is believed that humans hunted them to extinction. For a Mediterranean island to have supported an elephant population is quite a distinctive feature, and from Plato's description Cyprus and Atlantis seem to have shared very similar fauna.

Rivers and Lakes

According to Plato's Critias, all the animals and plants in Atlantis were able to thrive because fresh water was always available.

'for those which live in lakes and marshes and rivers, and also for those which live in mountains and on plains.'

Despite the modern general view of Cyprus as a dry island, it actually has many lakes, marshes and rivers. Akrotiri has a lake, as does Larnaka. You will find many marshes in the Famagusta area. Most of the rivers used to dry in the summer, but a few had water all year round. Today those rivers have been emptied almost at their sources for human consumption, either bottled or piped to fill reservoirs near big cities. But again, the ancient description matches both Cyprus and Atlantis.

Perfumes

In Critias, Plato speaks of lush and fragrant scents in Atlantis:

'Also whatever fragrant things there now are in the earth, whether roots, or herbage, or woods, or essences which distil from fruit and flower, grew and thrived in that land.'

The fact that he uses the word 'distil' is a clear indication that the island's roots, herbs and fruits were transformed by man, most probably into perfumes. In fact, the first perfumes known to man have been found at the Pyrgos Mavroraki site located close to Limasol in southern Cyprus. Perfume-making had been going on well before 2000 BC. The storage jars found there could hold 500 litres of oil, further indicating that this production was of a massive and commercial scale. Furthermore, this production was not limited to one type. Fourteen different types of residues, such as anise, pine, coriander, bergamot, almond and parsley, were found in that primordial factory.

Ancient perfume bottles have been found which date back to at least the time of the Trojan War. It was in the Homeric Hymns that we read:

> 'Aphrodite, lover of laughter,
> and a terrible passion seized her heart,
> she went away to Cyprus and she entered
> her fragrant temple at Paphos where she has
> her sanctuary and fragrant altar.
> There she went inside and closed
> The shining doors behind her.
> There the Graces bathed her and anointed her
> with heavenly oils, the kind the eternal gods always use,
> divinely sweet and filled with fragrance.'[30]

Even as recently as the 19th century a large number of products used in the making of perfumes seem to have names that derived from Cyprus: Cypriol (Cyperus Scariosus) and Oile Cyprinum. It therefore seems clear that the 'sweet scented stuff' of Atlantis was very similar to Aphrodite's perfumes.

Topography

In Critias, Plato calls Atlantis a 'very lofty' place:

> 'The whole country was said by him to be very lofty and precipitous on the side of the sea.'

That the island of Cyprus matches this 'lofty' description seems clear, as it possesses mountains rising nearly 2,000 metres. The Troodos range occupies most of the southern part of the island and seems to accord with Plato's description. The precipitous nature of Atlantis's coastline matches Cyprus, too. Apart from the eastern coast and some spots in the north, the whole island seems to be surrounded by cliffs all created by the colliding tectonic plates, also matching the description in Critias:

> 'but the country immediately about and surrounding the city was a level plain, itself surrounded by mountains which descended towards the sea; it was smooth and even, and of an oblong shape, extending in one direction three thousand stadia, but across the centre inland it was two thousand stadia.'

The level plain referred to here, clearly aligns with the Mesaoria plain that stretches from the Morphou Bay on the west, to the Famagusta district on the east and surrounded by mountains. On the south is the Troodos range and in the north is the Kyrenia range. The Kyrenia Mountains and Troodos range also seem to be descending towards the sea. The Kyrenia range also seems to be sheltering the plain from the northern winds, matching completely Plato's description:

> 'This part of the island looked towards the south, and was sheltered from the north. The surrounding mountains were

celebrated for their number and size and beauty, far beyond any which still exist, having in them also many wealthy villages of country folk.'

As for the beauty of the mountains and the wealth that still resides there, just a quick visit to the place today is enough to confirm the description.

A Major City

The Atlantis of Plato's description was home to a major ancient metropolis that would have been all but wiped away by the tsunami that hit the island. From the images of the tragic recent tsunamis we have seen, not only do cities often disappear completely, but even the landscapes surrounding the affected area change.

We all have this idea of the island of Atlantis at the bottom of the sea. But it is not clear that that was what Plato was telling us. He actually implies that it may still be visible in some parts. Plato writes in Critias that:

'For which reason the sea in those parts is impassable and impenetrable, because there is a shoal of mud in the way; and this was caused by the subsidence of the island.'

Plato is implying that the mud is visible. If the sea became impassable, it means that the sea must be very shallow. With a couple of metres' depth, a boat would have cleared the area. So if there is water it cannot be any deeper than 2 metres. This would make the town clearly still visible. The fact that he mentions mud surely means that we should look for some sort of wetland area.

Plato gave very clear measurements for the city of Atlantis. He mentioned that the first water circle was 3 stadia in width. The first land circle was 3 stadia too. Then you had another water area and land rings measuring 2 stadia each. The next circle was of water with a width of 1 stadia followed by the central island which was 5 stadia in diameter. Using the Attic measure of the stadia we get a diameter of the city of 2,500 metres with a central island of 925 metres' diameter. Looked on from above, using Google Earth, one can see how the Larnaka Salt Lake might have been circular before the flood. Superimposing these measurements with an image of the Salt Lake we can see that the northern shore seems to match the circumference exactly. In what would be the centre of the lake there is actually a religious building. The mosque of Hala Sultan Tekke is one of the most revered places in Islam. It is believed to be the resting place of the foster mother of the Prophet Mohammed. The site is built on top of an ancient cemetery from the Bronze Age that served a nearby city.

Fig. 2.2: Measurements of the city of Atlantis according to Plato over a Google Earth image.[31]

Recent excavations west of the mosque are uncovering what might have been the biggest city that ever existed in Cyprus during the Bronze Age. This seems to coincide with Plato's description of Atlantis. From the northern edge of the Salt Lake to the area of the mosque there is exactly the 2,500 metres that Plato calculated. In order to reach the excavation area, one has to cross a ditch, clearly reminiscent of and of similar size to the little canals described by Plato.

The size of the city the archaeologists have just started to excavate is believed to be at least 50 hectares in area—and work has only just begun. The actual excavations have already reached the period of 1600 BC and are nowhere near completion. Thus the possibility of finding more ancient remains is still open.

One of the first things a visitor notices is the canalization—proof that water was available and channelled for human use. There are also bathrooms, as mentioned by Plato. Furthermore, the existence of steps indicates that at least some buildings might have had two floors. Furthermore, the use of ashlar (a method of building which requires the stones cut to shape to fit the building) is a sign of luxury and architectural advancement rarely seen in buildings of the Bronze Age.

Archaeologists have also located some water sources. Four wells appear on the nearest elevation of land after reaching across a depression. It fits with the area where the second strip of land should be and where Plato located the fountains.

Four more findings stand out. First, a stone statue of a bull was found amid the ruins. Bulls were very commonly depicted in Cyprus and they had a predominant role in the life of Atlantis, according to Plato in Critias:

'There were bulls who had the range of the temple of Poseidon.'

The second was a temple of worship and a seashell of considerable size. This shell looks like an elongated snail and had been perforated on one side to become a sacred horn. This is a Triton shell, named after the son of Poseidon. Triton is often depicted holding one of these shells, which were often used for communicating.

The third discovery was found near the water line of the lake but over a mile from the sea—a large amount of anchor stones, which indicates that the area was a harbour during the Bronze Age. A piece of land that would have clearly been reached through canals is clearly the same situation that Atlantis reputedly had.

The final, and most remarkable find from the Salt Lake is now exhibited in the Cyprus Museum in Nicosia. It is a trident, elaborately crafted, probably not a working tool and clearly an item related to Poseidon, the god of Atlantis.

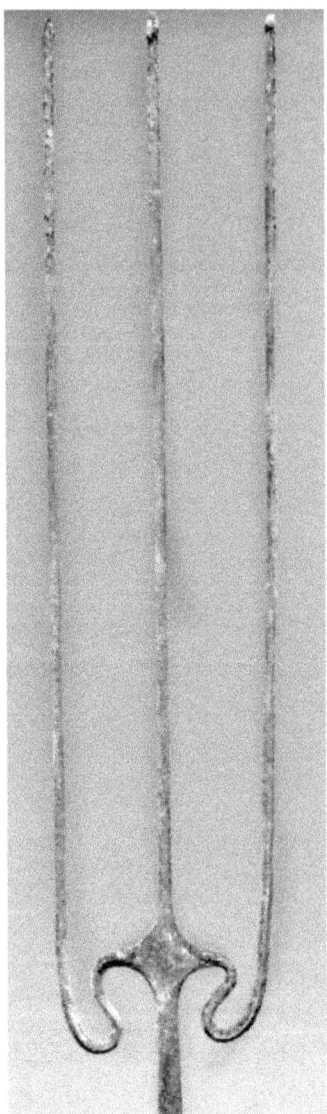

Fig. 2.3: Trident from Hala Sultan Tekke.[32]

The Salt Lake area is the only Bronze Age Cypriot city that had remains of a harbour situated inland served via canals. The name of the city is probably also recorded. In Ugarit they found references to a town in Cyprus called Atlg. We have also references to that city having a harbour.

'A ship from Ala [shiya...]
Which is in (the port of) Atlg....'[133]

Plato also says that a small sacred mount was located 50 stadia from the city. The sacred mountain of Stavrovouni stands a similar distance away from the Salt Lake area.

Festival of the Flood

Cyprus has a celebration that is unique. The Kataklysmos or Festival of the Flood is today a Christian celebration. It is celebrated every year, 50 days after the Orthodox Easter. During the celebrations the whole sea front is changed into an open market. There are singing competitions where the singers improvise the lyrics. They use no instruments and their origin goes back in time thousands of years. The songs are called Chatista, but the main celebrations have to do with water. After all, it is the Festival of the Flood.

As Robert Sarmast notes, the fact that this celebration is unique to Cyprus is proof that the island suffered a terrible flood. For sure the biblical story of the flood comes to mind, and one notices the similarities where a whole culture gets wiped out due to water. It now seems obvious why the city of Larnaka, the town built next to the remains of Atlantis, is where the day of the Kataklysmos or Festival of the Flood is most celebrated.

It is quite remarkable that the description of Atlantis given by Plato matches so closely the island of Cyprus. An island with all the physical attributes that Atlantis had, with a city-harbour matching the measurements given by Plato. A city with archaeological remains that seems to corroborate the idea of a maritime culture that could have controlled the seas. A land that the ancients acknowledged as an empire stretching across probably the whole of the Mediterranean

Sea and most of the areas around it. Just as Plato says, just as the Hebrew world knew it. A land that still celebrates a festival to commemorate the event that changed the world at the end of the Bronze Age.

So why do we know the town as Kition or Kittim and not Atlantida? The reason is quite simple: Kittim was the Hebrew name of the town. Phoenicians also knew it as Kition. But the Greek name would have been Atlantida. Atlantida meant daughter of Atlas and Atlas was the son of Iapetus. And with Iapetus is where the story overlaps. What the Greeks called Iapetus was called Japheth by the Hebrews. Kittim was the son of Javan who was the son of Japheth.

| *Iapetus* | father of | *Atlas* | father of | *Atlantida* |
| *Japheth* | father of | *Javan* | father of | *Kittim* |

Basically, Atlantida and Kittim are exactly the same. Both are second generation descendants of Iapetus/Japheth.

After the end of the Bronze Age the town was colonied by the Phoenicians and the Phoenician name of the town is what prevailed. But Plato was Greek. A Greek in a very proud Greek nation. He had to use the less known but Greek name of the town. This seems to be validated by Plato himself when he writes in Critias that:

'Yet, before proceeding further in the narrative, I ought to warn you, that you must not be surprised if you should perhaps hear Hellenic names given to foreigners. I will tell you the reason of this: Solon, who was intending to use the tale for his poem, enquired into the meaning of the names, and found that the early Egyptians in writing them down had translated them into their own language, and he recovered the meaning of the several names and when copying them out again translated them into our language.'

Chapter 3
THE ISLAND OF THE GODS

In this chapter we will show evidence of the existence of the same gods as the Greek developed in the 8th century present in Cyprus during the Bronze Age. We should also find temples and proof of worship of the same gods at least a thousand years prior to their arrival in Greece. We will also try to explain the Titans which according to ancient writers were the origin of the gods and one of their fiercest enemies. We will try to reconcile the Greek mythology with Titan geography.

In Plato's story, it is clear that the Atlanteans worshipped the same gods as in ancient Greece. He does not mention the names of all the gods, but Poseidon, the god of Atlantis, was always one of the 12 Gods that gathered on Mount Olympus. Plato also says that:

'Zeus, the god of gods ... collected all the gods into their most holy habitation....'

It can then be deduced that the other gods were the rest of the 'Greek' Olympians, as myths would not make sense with Poseidon and Zeus but without Athena, Aphrodite, Apollo and the rest. Plato then says that:

'In the days of old, the gods had the whole earth distributed among them by allotment.'

If Cyprus is the island of Atlantis and the gods divided the land between themselves, there should be indications of these divisions. Of course the division of the island into ten kingdoms is not arbitrary. Those divisions seem to fit the arrangements of the Olympians. Zeus and Hera were the hosts at Mount Olympus, and the ten other gods joined them there. The ten kings of Atlantis were believed to be descendants of these gods. Similarly, in each of the kingdoms in Cyprus there is always one god that seems predominant. Apollo is clearly the god of the kingdom of Kourion and Aphrodite is the goddess of Paphos.

Aphrodite

There is a special connection between Aphrodite and Adonis and the ancient kingdom of Paphos. Aphrodite was one of the most important goddesses in antiquity, representing love, pleasure and procreation. According to myth, her birth was due to the conflict between two Titans. When Cronos severed Uranus's genitals and threw them into the sea, Aphrodite rose from the foam. That is the reason she was given the name Aphrodite by the Greeks, which means 'foam-arisen'. Hesiod describes her conception in Theogony as:

'Great Heaven came, bringing on the night, and, desirous of love, he spread himself over Earth, stretched out in every direction. His son reached out from the ambush with his left hand; with his right he took the huge sickle with its long row of sharp teeth and quickly cut off his father's genitals, and flung them behind him to fly where they might...

As for the genital, just as he first cut them off with his instrument of adamant and threw them from the land into the surging sea, even so they were carried on the waves for a long time. About them a white foam grew from the immortal flesh, and in it a girl formed. First she approached holy Cythera; then from there she came to sea-girt Cyprus. And out stepped a modest and beautiful goddess, and the grass began to grow all round beneath her slender feet. Gods and men call her Aphrodite, because she was formed in foam, and Cytherea, because she approached Cythera, and Cyprus-born, because she was born in wave-washed Cyprus, and "genial" because she appeared out of genitals. Eros and fair Desire attended her birth and accompanied her as she went to join the family of gods. And this has been her allotted province from the beginning among men and immortal gods.'[134]

In all accounts she became one of the 12 Olympians right from the start. There is no account of her having a childhood. She seems to have appeared as an adult—and a very sexually desirable one indeed. Most accounts agree that her home was in Paphos, a town situated in the southwest part of Cyprus. That is the reason why she was also called 'Cyprian'. The ancient city of Paphos was actually not in modern-day Paphos but 16 kilometres south, in the village of Kouklia. Today a town with not many inhabitants, but many more people must have lived there in antiquity, as there is evidence of at least 100 hectares of human activity. The first signs of human inhabitation in the centre of the town dates from the late Bronze Age.

At around 1200 BC we see the first sign of a temple of Aphrodite in Kouklia, the earliest temple of Aphrodite ever found. It predates any temple of Aphrodite in Greece by more than 400 years. The temple consisted of a one-level rectangular building made out of large ashlar stones. The measurements were probably 27 metres long by 9 metres wide. The temple had a sacred enclosure at the front surrounded by massive limestone blocks. The walls were known as Cyclopean, as it was believed that only giants like the Cyclops could have moved them. On top of the temple were masonry 'horns', which today are known as horns of consecration. The sacred enclosure, also referred to as temenos, contained an altar and a water basin. The main building, or holy of holies, was divided by a row of square pillars. This was the area where only the head priest could enter.

From recent archaeological excavations we know that the worship of a goddess of fertility in Cyprus started as early as 9500 BC. Since the worshippers must have gathered somewhere, we can expect that they must have had temples or places of worship well before 1200 BC. The actual temples have not been located but clay models of them have appeared all around the island.

Fig. 3.1: Clay shrine of Kotchati.[35]

This clay model of a shrine found at Kotchati seems to depict exactly what experts believed the temple in Kouklia would have looked like, with the horns of consecration, the holy of holies divided by a middle square pillar, and with the priest at the front next to the holy basin. This shrine is from the middle Bronze Age (c. 1700 BC), 500 years earlier than the temple at Kouklia. This shrine is not unique as there are other clay figures depicting exactly the same temple shrine.

A different version was found in a bowl found in a tomb near Bellapais, and it gives the most astonishing depiction of what was actually going on in the sacred enclosure. Called the Vounous Bowl, it has been dated to around 2000 BC.

Fig. 3.2: Vounous Bowl.[36]

The bowl represents the temenos or sacred enclosure, with its main gate, some sacred animals and a king/head priest sitting on a throne. If you look at the opposite side from the entrance, you see that the person sitting at the throne is facing a structure that seems structurally very similar to the shrine of Kotchati.

V.T.22-26

But there are even older representations of this temenos. In Kissonerga near the modern town of Paphos, archaeologists have unearthed a bowl with seemingly no other purpose but to depict a shrine. The bowl had a movable aperture, appearing to render it unusable as a container for anything else.

Fig. 3.4: Kissonerga Bowl.[38]

The temple seems to date back to the Chalcolitic era, as the site of Kissonerga lasted from 3500 BC until it was abandoned in 2500 BC, predating the temples found in Greece by nearly two thousand years.

Adonis

Aphrodite's favourite lover, Adonis, was the god of beauty who would die and resurrect. Like his paramour, he was also born in Cyprus, the son of the Paphian king Cinyras. The story is told by many Greek writers, including Hyginus:

'Venus (Aphrodite) later pitied her (Smyrna, who she had caused to lie with her father Kinyras), and changed her into a kind of tree from which myrrh flows; Adonis, born from it, exacted punishment for his mother's sake from Venus.'

The actual place where Adonis lived is not as well known as that of Aphrodite, but in 1910 it was discovered by German archaeologist Dr Max Ohnefalsch-Richter. The site was so rich in finds, having signs of many gods, that it was called 'a real Mount Olympus' by the Daily Mail. The New York Times wrote: *'The Gods clubhouse has been found in Cyprus.'* The news even reached New Zealand, where the Northern Advocate reported a *'Mountain of the Gods'.*

It was obvious that it was a major discovery, but unfortunately there were problems keeping the site safe from looters. The New York Times reported in their article that: 'Dr Richter has been hampered, of course, by the ignorance and dishonesty of the "illicit diggers" who abound in Cyprus. The excavation laws of the island are very strict, but they are constantly evaded.'[39]

When the site was finally excavated, they found a major worship complex with many chambers carved from the rock. Around the temple complex they found nearly 200 inscriptions in Cipro-syllabic script which, at the time, had yet to be deciphered. Cypriot sanctuaries of this period typically contain quantities of votive statuary, often in great abundance, as did the site at Rantidi:

'In any single one of the rooms of typical image sanctuaries which abound in the island hundreds of entire statues and statuettes have invariably been found, sculptured or modelled out of stone, marble, or clay, or bronze, and varying from the most colossal dimensions to the smallest size. And thousands of fragments are found in each spot, if we number each piece separately, as the government authorities did at Rantidi.'[40]

The finds were prolific, but unfortunately many appear to have been lost. Some of the recovered artefacts are held by the Cyprus Museum in Nicosia, where they remain somewhere deep in the vaults and not on public display.

Since 1910, much more has been revealed about the site. We know that Adonis was worshipped at the temple as early as the Archaic Age around 700 BC, but human activity in the area dates from at least the Chalcolithic era. The sanctuary both contains and is surrounded by numerous tombs. These findings support the connection with Adonis, the god of death and resurrection.

The fact that the site is visible from the town of Kouklia seems to accord with the myth. Adonis would not be far from the town of his father or the place where his lover lived.

The couple became one of the most worshipped gods in Cyprus. When Ohnefalsch-Richter published his book Kypros, the Bible and Homer: Oriental civilization, art and religion in ancient times, he recorded numerous sanctuaries of Aphrodite and Adonis all around the island and the rest of the world.

In his introduction to the book, Ohnefalsch-Richter wrote:

'From Cyprus Aphrodite and Adonis started on their triumphal progress through the ancient world.'

Their story with some little changes would also go viral.

The Olympians were so called because they lived on top of Mount Olympus. Today the tallest mountain in Cyprus is called Mount Olympus. Situated in the Troodos range, it measures 1,952 metres. In Homer's Iliad and in Hesiod's Theogony, Mount Olympus appeared as 'Chionides' or 'snowy peaks'—i.e., plural. So it cannot be a single mount; it must be a range like the Troodos range.

In the Odyssey, however, Homer describes Olympus as:

'where people say the gods have made their everlasting home. Shaken by no wind, drenched by no showers, and invaded by no snows, it is set in cloudless limpid air with a white radiance playing over all.'[41]

This Mount Olympus seems to fit a single mount in a very dry place. Homer makes clear that this Mount Olympus is the one where the gods lived. It describes a single mount with a conical shape situated in the vicinity of Kition, modern day Larnaca. The mountain later received the name of Stavrovouni due to the fact that Empress Helena, mother of Constantine the Great, in 327 AD, left there a part of the cross on which Jesus was crucified. The name Stavrovouni means 'mountain of the cross'. Stavrovouni would be then the main candidate as the one described in the Odyssey. It seems clear that it is the Cypriot Olympus when he writes:

'Hermes went off through the island forest making for high Olympus.'[42]

There is no Mount Olympus anywhere in the world located on an island but Cyprus. Further evidence comes from mythology. Mount Olympus was described as a temple where Zeus kept an eternal flame that was stolen by Prometheus in order to give fire to mankind. In the myth, the Titan Prometheus went to Mount Olympus on a day that they performed ritual offerings to the gods, consisting of animal parts thrown to the eternal fire of Olympus, and tricked Zeus.

'But the noble son of Iapetos (Prometheus) outwitted him by stealing the far-beaconing flare of untiring fire in the tube of fennel.'[43]

Iapetos who was the father of Atlas, founder of Atlantis links both myths. The 'untiring fire' seems to coincide with the much later legend of Empress Helena and the founding of the monastery Stavrovouni, which was built on top of a pagan temple. A stone found in the monastery links the ancient temple to Zeus, and legend says that Helena, shipwrecked in Cyprus, left the cross and built a chapel at the top of the hill 'where a bright light was coming out of the peak'. The bright light could be explained by a ceremonial fire, similar to the eternal flame of myth. This seems to support the claim of Stavrovouni as the original Mount Olympus.

Titans and Giants

Genetic study indicates that the people who brought the Neolithic to the world were not originally from Cyprus but from the mainland. That might accord with mythology, where the Gods are descendants of the Titans. Could it be that all the areas of the mainland around Cyprus were what they were referring to by Titans?

Once you look at the toponymy of locations in antiquity, you might certainly begin to believe that.

Uranos was the husband of Mother Earth. He represented the sky and the origin of all creatures. Together with Mother Earth they produced all the Titans and from them came the gods. If the sky was to be represented in any area of the planet, it would be in the highest mountains. The highest mountains of the area are the Caucasus.

The most notorious peak of the Caucasus area is Mount Ararat, a mountain made famous by Christianity as the landing spot of Noah's Ark after the great flood described in Genesis. That area is where the ancient kingdom of Urartu was located. Another kingdom called Ur appeared, which descended from the high mountains to settle in the area of Mesopotamia. Descending from the heights is a good reason why the ancient Greeks called it the land of the Hurrians or Uranos.

Next to the land of Uranos is the land of Mother Earth: Gaia. To locate this land, you need to find its most famous produce: The Golden Apples of the Hesperides. Today it is difficult to believe that some apples made out of gold grew from trees. But that was not the case. The 'apples' were a real fruit, but when the myths were transferred from Cyprus to Greece they lost their real meaning. Only in Cyprus do people refer to a real fruit called the Golden Apple. The fruit called berikokia in Greece, apricot in English, is called chrysomilo in Cyprus, which literally translates as golden apples. So where is the land of the golden apples? If you ask the Romans, and many botanists, they will tell you that they originated in the Armenia area. The fruit's scientific name is Prunus armenica, which translates to 'Armenian prune'. Thus, the Hesperides likely refers to Armenia.

Ladon, believed to be one of Gaia's sons by Uranos, was the serpent-like dragon that twined and twisted around the tree in the Garden of the Hesperides and guarded the golden apples. According to Greek mythology, Heracles killed Ladon as part of his 12 labours. The following day, Jason and the Argonauts passed by on their return journey from Colchis and heard the lament of 'shining' Aegle, one of the four Hesperides, and viewed the still-twitching Ladon. The legend of Ladon and his relation to the Argonautica places the land of the Hesperides near Colchis, a land that was clearly on the Asian side of the Black Sea or Pontus Euxinus.

Since the Armenian genocide of 1915–1917 the area has been under Turkish control. The changes in various town names through history still seem to indicate the actual location of the Hesperides. A town called Ispir was at some point called Speri or Sper. Herodotus called the people from that area Saspirians, and during Roman times the area was called Hispiratis. It seems very likely that this is the place that the Greeks referred to as the Hesperides—especially considering that the main produce and biggest export of that area are still today the apricots or golden apples.

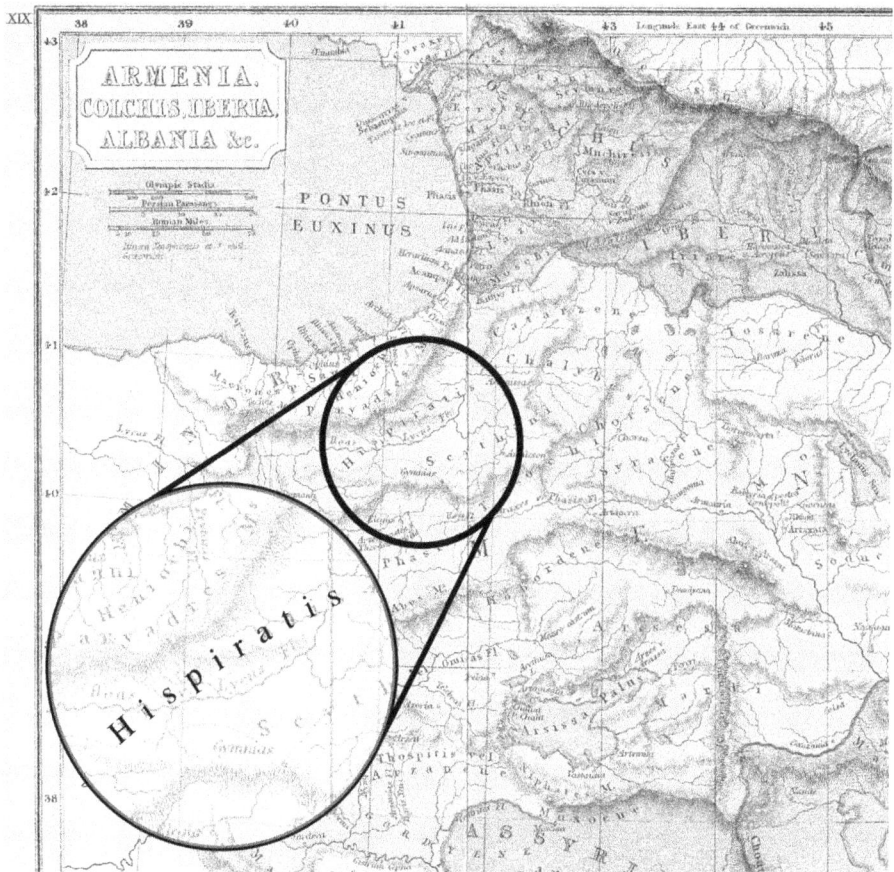

Fig. 3.5: Detail of 19th century map showing Hispiratis.[44]

When Aphrodite was born from the castration of Uranos, she took with her some golden apples from Hesperides. Ancient writers such as Ovid noted that the golden apples had made it to Cyprus before their time:

> 'The people call the close of Tamasus,
> The richest part of all the isle of Cyprus,
> Which long ago was hallowed in my name
> And added as endowment to my shrine.
> A tree stands in the close with leaves of gold
> And golden branches rustling in the breeze.
> On my way thence it chanced that in my hand

> *I held three golden apples I had picked
> And I stood by Hippomenes, unseen
> Except by him, and taught the apples use.*[44]

There seems little doubt that the golden apples from Armenia ended up in Cyprus.

The Titan of the Sea was called Pontus. The area next to Hispiratis towards the Black Sea was called Pontus Euxinus by the Romans—or, the 'people of Pontus'. Pontus meant sea and the 'Euxinus' derived from 'friendly to foreigners'. But 'friendly to foreigners' was a new term used after the 4th century BC. Before that the sea was 'inhospitable'—as attested by the story of Jason and the Argonauts. Pindar calls it Pontus axeinos in the Pythian Ode 4.

Helios is related to the area of southwest Anatolia. The Iliad cites Helios as on the side of the Trojans. In later days the worship of Helios centred in the island of Rhodes. It was there that the biggest statue of Helios ever built was found. The statue, called the Collosus of Rhodes, was one of the 'Seven Wonders of the World'.

From the southern area of Anatolia also came the mother of Apollo, the Titan Leto. The centre of Leto worship was the town of Letoon just south of the town of Fethiye in what used to be the kingdom of Lycia.

In ancient Greece and Rome, they knew that the area we now call Israel was the land of Cronus or El as they called their god. All the lands from Hazor to Ashkelon were part of the lands of Cronus. The people of Israel still today take their day of rest on the day of Cronus (Saturn)—Saturday.

The Titan Perses clearly refers to the area known as Persia. The myth of Perseus is always linked to Medusa, who is in turn linked to Medea and the land of the Medes. Medea was the daughter of the king of

Colchis in the Black Sea, who left her land and went to a land that would become the area called Media, in what is now Iran.

The Titans were sent to Tartarus by Zeus. The name Tartarus is still used today and relates to an area beyond the land of the Arians. Still today there is an ethnic group called the Tatars. The Tatars were the people that gave us tartar sauce and steak tartare. At that time, their land extended all the way to Turkmenistan, and it is there that you find one of its features: the pits of Tartarus. The pits where Titans and other people alike were sent as a punishment, and today, the pits, are still visible. The area is called the Karakum desert, and it features numerous natural sinkholes produced by the collapse of the gas deposits below. Some of them formed recently due to human intervention. Other pits have existed since ancient times. But the legend goes that the punishment was for victims to have their guts eaten by vultures. It was Herodotus who would record for history for the first time the real tartarus pits of mythology. Herodotus explains how the people of the area were using for funerary purposes what would later be called the tower of silence—a small tower with a pit in the centre. Bodies of the dead would be placed on top of the tower for vultures to eat until the bones were clean. The bones would then be thrown in the pit so that they would not contaminate water or earth. Towers of silence would be found in any area where Zoroastrianism was prevalent, but the oldest one known is found in the village of Nukus in Uzbekistan, right in the area identified as Tartarus.

Fig. 3.6: Water crater in Karakum desert.⁴⁵

Typhon was the biggest monster of Greek mythology and the father of all monsters. The place to locate this monster is the Orontes River. The river was called Typhon and Drako during antiquity. Strabo explains:

'The Orontes River flows near the city. This river has its sources in Coelê-Syria; and then, after flowing underground, issues forth again; and then, proceeding through the territory of the Apameians into that of Antiocheia, closely approaches the latter city and flows down to the sea near Seleuceia. Though formerly called Typhon, its name was changed to that of Orontes, the man who built a bridge across it.'⁴⁶

This is the same Typhon that Zeus defeated at a place named Arima, which was also known as the couch of Typhon. The place is now known as the Corycian Cave and is situated in the coastal Turkish city of Corycos.

The next Titan is probably the most important. Atlas was the leader of the Titans during the Titanomachy. What we know as Atlas, is what the people from central Anatolia called Hatti. The people of Hatti became Atlas in Greek mythology. In the Bible they are called the Hittites. Many names have preserved the Atl- origin within the Anatolia area. One of the biggest cities in southern Anatolia is called Antalia. One of the most common male names used by Turks is Attila. One of the most famous kings of Pergamon (Turkey) was called Attalus and there was a dynasty of the Attalids. Even the name Anatolia seems to come from that same root.

So it seems clear that the Titans represented the great powers on the continent, and that their offspring, the Olympian gods, were much more connected to Cyprus than to Greece.

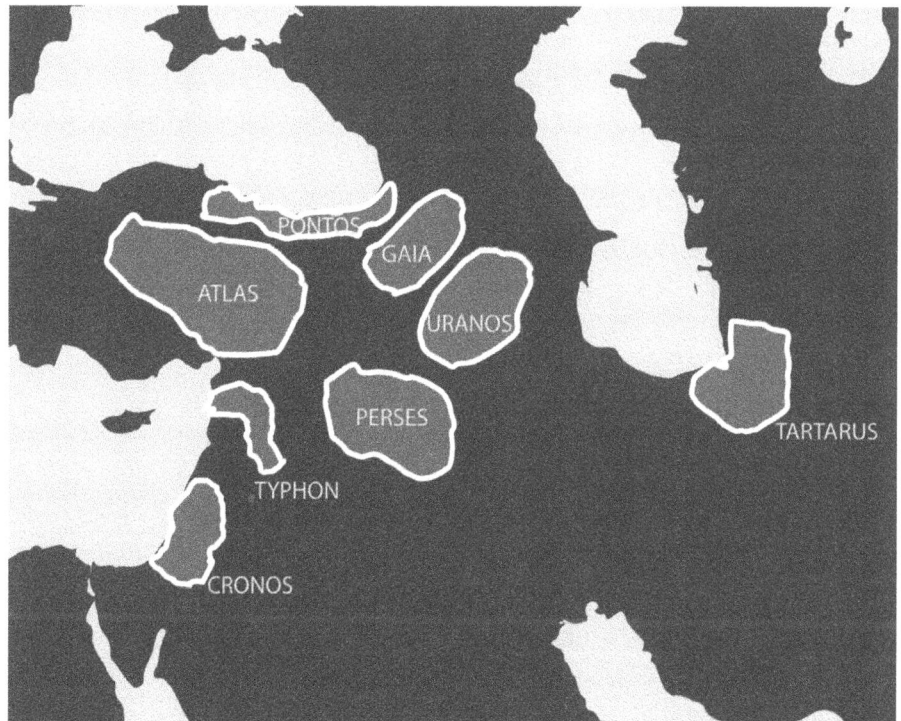

Fig. 3.7: Titans locations.[47]

The Island of the Gods

Cyprus fits the physical description of the land where the Gods lived. It has the Mount Olympus where they met, and the land was divided between the gods. Out of the 12 Olympians, we have Zeus and Hera that live on Mount Olympus. The other ten had land allocated to them and had their meetings at the sacred mountain. Ten kingdoms living in harmony, with each one of them ruled by a king who was also the high priest of the god. Exactly as it was in Cyprus, exactly as it was in Atlantis.

This certainly makes much more sense than what we have been made to believe from Greece. Gods that had to live in a land above the clouds and they had to descend to a Mount Olympus, with no archaeological remains at all, and gather there. They had to fly to reach each other as they all lived on separate islands. They came down from the clouds to have sexual relations with mortals and then go back to the clouds. But even more complicated was for the heroes as they were supposed to be originally mortals that became semi-gods. Therefore, they had to be able to join the gods in their unbelievable flying achievements.

Certainly the idea of a high priest-king as representative of the gods living in different parts of the island makes more sense. The heroes were humans that reached a high level of achievement and popular respect which qualified them to join the gods in their temples or at the top of Mount Olympus in Stavrovouni. Today we still do this. In Barcelona, where I am from, Lionel Messi is our hero. Some people actually describe him as a football god. Ancient people doing the same would not surprise anyone.

From all this we can deduce that the island's mythology had a far earlier origin than the Greek mythology. The earlier origin of the gods seems to be confirmed by the ancient writers. Ovid wrote a text called The Ages of Men within the Metamorphose, in which he divides the history of mankind based on the much earlier texts of Hesiod. According to Ovid, the Ages of Men were four—gold, silver, bronze and Iron. He writes that the Golden Age was when the Rule of Cronos and men did not know agriculture. He explained hunter-gatherer cultures as:

> *'Earth willingly, untouched, unwounded yet*
> *By hoe or plough, gave all her bounteous store;*
> *Men were content with nature's food unforced,*
> *And gathered strawberries on the mountainside*
> *And cherries and the clutching bramble's fruit,*
> *And accorns fallen from Jove's spreading tree.'*
> *He also explains those first seafaring cultures:*
> *'No Pine had yet, on its high mountain felled,*
> *Descended to the sea to find strange lands*
> *Afar; men knew no shores except their own.'*

Zeus already existed but his rule would start in the Silver Age. It seems likely that the Silver Age would have started with those first boats trips going out of Cyprus and the beginning of the rule of Zeus, suggesting that these stories originated at the dawn of agriculture on the island of Cyprus.

Chapter 4
TROY AND HOMER

There is still an issue that needs to be resolved to be convinced that the island of Atlantis and the island of Cyprus are one and the same. Historians have been telling us that the events of the end of the Bronze Age were a conflict between a confederation known as the Sea People and the rest of the world. On the other hand, we have literature where Homer describes the events of the Bronze Age collapse as triggered by the Greeks, led by Agamemnon, king of Mycenae, against the Anatolian kingdom of Troy, led by King Priam and his sons Paris and Hector. On the other hand, mythology tells us that the Titanomachy was the battle that ended that Bronze Age. Is there a way to reconcile all three? Could it be that history, literature and mythology were different versions of the same events?

Could it be that the story of Atlantis was an incomplete account of those same events?
But before we try to reconcile that, we need to address a major issue that could help clarify some misunderstandings.

Do the stories written in the 8th century have any historical value to explain events from 400 years earlier? Oral transmission of the stories would have rendered them unrecognizable as "Chinese Whispers" demonstrates. The only hope to get some real history from those early texts, is if the transmission was written. To support that theory, we need to see who and how could have done that transmission.

The period that followed the Trojan War is something of a mystery. Historians call this period the Greek Dark Ages. During this period, the area we now call Greece suffered a high depopulation and the total disappearance of any palaces or religious buildings. The few remaining people likely endured a near subsistence economy. Until the appearance of the Greek alphabet in the 8th century, there is actually no record of any writing, in any language, happening in the area of the Aegean.

In his book Homer and His Forerunners, C.M. Bowra puts the problem in straightforward terms:

> *'There is no evidence whatsoever that the Mycenaean script continued anywhere in Greece after c. 1200. There is no trace of writing of any kind in the sub-Mycenaean and Protogeometric periods, or indeed before the middle of the eighth century, when the new and totally different Greek alphabet makes its first appearance. Now, this is surely not an accident. A single scratched letter from this period would be enough to show that writing survived; but not one has been found. This is undeniably a most remarkable phenomenon, for which it is hard to find either a parallel or an explanation. A society seems suddenly to have become illiterate, and to have remained so for centuries. How and why this happened we do not know.'* [48]

That raises a question, which has puzzled many historians. As 20th-century mythology scholar Immanuel Velikovsky has pointed out, the Battle of Troy was supposed to have happened at the beginning of the 12th century BC, around 1190 BC. If Homer wrote the Iliad, narrating the story of the battle around 750 BC, how do we know about the stories of the Battle of Troy? How were the stories transmitted for 450 years?

The first theory was that the Battle of Troy simply never happened and Homer's story was fiction. After all, many had assumed the city of Troy was just a myth until it was discovered in 1868 by Heinrich Schliemann. He eventually found a layer with the signs of a major battle dated to the beginning of the 12th century BC. He found evidence of destruction by fire and great loss of life, just as Homer's Iliad told us. Troy was real, and it seems that the events that Homer described actually did happen.

Could it be that the story was transmitted orally until Homer wrote it down? This option seems unlikely as the people who would tell the stories would be professional court jesters, and courts were something that did not appear to have existed in the Aegean during those years. Another issue that seems to point to a written transmission of the events is the descriptions of some places, like sandy Pylos, stunningly accurate. Homer also talks about certain cities that actually did not survive the war, some in the Aegean, some in Anatolia; some on Agamemnon's side, some on Priam's side—cities that did not exist at the time of Homer and would remain so until they were unearthed by archaeologists. The distorting effects of oral transmission would likely have altered some details or omitted them entirely.
Thus, the question remains: How did Homer know about the Battle of Troy? Could it be that the stories were transmitted in the area of Anatolia?

The answer seems clear; Anatolia suffered a similar fate, perhaps even worse than the Aegean. Immanuel Velikovsky looked at the possibility and wrote:

> *'Like Greece and the Aegean, Asia Minor has no history for a period of close to five centuries. Certain scholars disagree with this verdict, but it comes from the pen of one of the foremost*

authorities on archaeology and art of Asia Minor, Professor Ekrem Akurgal of the University of Ankara.
... Today [1961], despite all industrious archaeological exploration of the last decades, the period from 1200 to 750 for most parts of the Anatolian region lies still in complete darkness. The old nations of Asia Minor, like the Lycians and the Carians, the names of which are mentioned in the documents of the second half of the second millennium, are archaeologically, i.e., with their material heritage, first noticeable about 700 or later... Hence the cultural remains of the time between 1200 and 750 in central Anatolia, especially on the plateau, seem to be quite irretrievably lost for us.

The huge land of Asia Minor for almost five centuries is historically and archaeologically void. The cause of the interruption in the flow of history about -1200 is assumed to lie in some military conquest; but the Phrygians, who are supposed to have been these conquerors, did not themselves leave any sign of their occupation of the country between 1200 and 750.

Thus the explanation that the end of the Anatolian civilization about 1200 was due to the incursion of the Phrygians is not supported by archaeological finds. According to Akurgal, the repeatedly undertaken efforts to close the hiatus by relics of Phrygian art "cannot be harmonized with the results of archaeological study. None of the Phrygian finds and none of the oriental ones found with them can be dated earlier than the eighth century." "Such results compel us to exclude from the study of Asia Minor between 1200 and 750 any Phrygian presence and heritage."

If there is no sign of Phrygian occupation for the period, are there possibly some vestiges of occupation by other peoples?
"It is startling," writes Akurgal, "that until now in Central Anatolia not only no Phrygian, but altogether no cultural remains of any people, came to light that could be dated in time between 1200 and 750." Nothing was left by any possible survivors of previous

occupants, namely by Hittites, and nothing by any people or tribe that could have supplanted them. Also on the rim of Asia Minor the darkness of the Dark Age is complete: "In the south of the peninsula, in Mersin, Tarsus and Karatepe, in recent years important archaeological work was done ... here, too, the early Iron Age, i.e., the period between 1200 and 750, is enwrapped in darkness."⁴⁹

As Scottish historian Emmet John Sweeney points out:

'this "darkness" did not represent a period of impoverishment or barbarism, but one of complete and total depopulation: a span of over four centuries when it seemed no human beings at all had existed in the region we now call Turkey.'⁵⁰

When we consider the evidence, there are no other candidates for the transmission of the stories in the so-called Greek world than Cyprus.

Cyprus not only did not suffer any depopulation but also had a written language during the period of the Greek Dark Ages. So how would the Cypriots know the stories of the battle and all the locations where it took place? This could only have happened if the people that took part in the Trojan War were actually from Cyprus or lived in Cyprus. The answer is given by Cypriot mythology and seems to be confirmed by archaeology. During the period that followed the Battle of Troy, a great number of people migrated from the Aegean to Cyprus. Numerous cities seem to appear in the island and mythology gives us the names of the people that created them.

Agapenor was the king of the Arcadian city Tegea. The son of Ancaeus and grandson of Lycurgus, Agapenor, landed in Cyprus following a great storm. The place where he and his men set foot on the island was near the town of Kouklia, where they founded the town of Paphos. An epigraph on the grave of Agapenor refers to him as the king of Paphos:

'Here lies master Agapenor, son of Ancaeus, king of Paphos.'

Cepheus, the brother of Lycurgus, also settled in Cyprus. With his men he built the city of Kyrenia on the northern coast. The same Cepheus sailed with Jason and the other Argonauts to Colchis, accompanied by his 20 sons, and later helped Heracles in his campaign against Hippocoon.

Many other Greeks came too. Praxandros, from the area around Sparta, settled just a few miles from Kyrenia in the city of Lapithos. Argives built the city of Kourion on a hill by the sea on the southern coast, just east of the temple of Apollo Hylates. Agamemnon was supposed to have come to Cyprus to remove Kinyras from Amathus and give the area to his comrades. Akamas, son of Theseus, came with his brother Demophon and founded the city of Aipeia, later called Soli. Chytrus, grandson of Akamas, founded the city of Chytri, present-day Kythrea. Teucer, half-brother to Ajax the Great, founded the city of Salamis.
But not only Greeks came to Cyprus. Chalcanor was a descendant of King Priam of Troy. When he arrived on the island looking for a place to settle, he went to a temple of Apollo near Chytri and asked the oracle where he should settle. The oracle answered:

'Your city must be built at the place where you see the sun rise in the morning hours.'

They travelled south until the morning. Then, one of Chalcanor's comrades climbed a hill and shouted: 'My king, idon alion' ('I saw the sun'). They decided to build the city on top of that hill, and that is the location of Idalion.

The influx of new settlers in the wake of the Trojan War seems obvious if you consider Cyprus as the motherland of all the people taking part in the battle. If they all originated from Atlantis, or Cyprus as we call it today, it makes sense that in times of trouble they would all rally at the centre of their vast empty.

The Greek Alphabet

Another key clue to the Cypriot origin of the ancient Greeks stories lies in the Greek alphabet. The Greek alphabet has been proven to stem from the Phoenician alphabet. This is no surprise as most of the Greek culture seems to come from the east.

Just looking at the Phoenician alphabet it becomes clear that this was the case. The words for 'ox', 'house', 'camel' and 'door' in Phoenician are pronounced as alf, beth, gaml and delt and have a clear resemblance to alpha, beta, gamma and delta. The actual symbols are also very similar.

The Bavarian-born Professor of Classics at the University of Zurich, Walter Burkert writes in his book The Orientalizing Revolution:

'There is much to substantiate the idea that Cyprus had a role to play as an intermediary station in the transmission of writing: The distinctive designation of the Greek letters as Phoinikeia seems to presuppose that other "scribblings" (grammata) were known from which the Phoenicians were different. This was the case only in Cyprus, where a linear script of Mycenean type had been adapted to the Greek and persisted to Hellenistic times; the first document now known for its use in writing Greek dates from the eleventh century.'[51]

Before the 'Phoinikeia grammata', there were other scripts in the Aegean. They are called Linear A, Linear B, and the Cypro-Minoan. These types of letters are all believed to be of oriental origin.

Linear A dates from the beginning of the second millennium and seems to have originated from a Semitic area and travelled through Anatolia to Crete. This language seems to have been the one utilized by the Minoan culture and disappeared after the explosion of the Santorini Caldera. Unsurprisingly, Linear A was very similar to the language used in Cyprus (Cypro-Minoan). It seems reasonable to think that the language spoken by the Minoans could have also come from Cyprus. Linear B is the next language known in Greece. It seems to start around 1450 BC and to disappear by the end of the Mycenaean culture around 1100 BC. Cypro-Minoan seems to have originated around 1550 BC and by 1050 BC transformed into the Cypriot Syllabary, which was used well into the 4th century BC. The same relation that Linear A had with the Cypro-Minoan seems to follow with Linear B and the Cypriot Syllabary; they all seem to share a common origin. It then makes more sense that the languages that were spoken in Greece would have originated in Cyprus and then travelled to Greece rather than the other way round.

All these languages appear to be scripts for a language that was some form of ancient Greek. But Cyprus was the only place that maintained the use of a written language during the Dark Ages in Greece offering

the necessary continuity for the development of a language.
The transition from the Cypro-Minoan into the Phoinikeia Grammata occurred at around 1050 BC. The transition probably occurred in the area of Amathus, as it was there that most of the inscriptions in the new language were found. Paphos and Amathus are where most pre-Greek finds have been made, where all the statues of the pre-Greek fertility goddesses have been found, suggesting that the Greek language originated in Cyprus. If the new language had been imported from Greece, it would have been found in cities of stronger Greek influence and not in the most pre-Greek Cypriot cities. It can also be deduced that the adaptation of the alphabet was an ongoing process that can only have happened in Cyprus, where the Phoenician and Greek cultures had been living side by side at least since the 14th century BC.

So the language that the alphabet served, must have been the language spoken by the people living in Cyprus. This does not exclude the possibility that the people living in Greece would also speak that same language, but it seems clear that the Greek alphabet was created in Cyprus for a language that was spoken in Cyprus. The other option is to believe that the Greek alphabet was created by people that could neither read nor write.

If the language and the people telling the stories were from Cyprus, could it be that the most famous Greek writer of all time could also have been Cypriot?

Homer the Cypriot

Homer has always been identified as one of the first Greek writers, but there is a lot of evidence to suggest that he was more Cypriot than Greek.

Epiphanios of Salamis wrote:

'How many persons say any number of things of Homer? Some claim he was Egyptian- others, that he was from Chios; others from Colophon; others a Phrygian. Others, Meletus and Critheidus, say that he came from Smyrna. Aristarchus [of Samothrace,3rd/ 2nd c. B.C.] declared him an Athenian, others a Lydian from Maeon, others, a Cypriote from Propoetis, a district near Salamis. Yet Homer was a man, surely! But because of his visits to many countries, he has impelled many to give different descriptions of him.'[52]

In the 4th-5th century AD there were already many doubts as to where Homer came from. Many areas claim Homer as its citizen, including Egypt, Athens, Phrygia, Colophon, Chios, Maeon—and Cyprus. The claim that he was Egyptian is the easiest to dismiss as there is nothing that links him with that land. He might have travelled to Egypt and certainly knew things about that land, but there is no other reason to link him to Egypt. After all, he wrote in Greek. The claim to Athens is also difficult to sustain. The language that he wrote in is quite different to the Athenian variant of Greek. There is no evidence of him having travelled to Athens either.

The only plausible options are either Anatolia or Cyprus. Let us examine the Anatolian claim first.
Chios, Smyrna, Miletus, Ephesus and Halicarnassus have all claimed Homer at some point. We also see temples dedicated to Homer like the one in Smyrna described by Strabo. But none of these places claim to be his birthplace. You would not have a temple built in your honour before your works were well known, unless you were famous for other reasons. It is also difficult to believe that he was from an area with no evidence of any writing, and hardly any people, for nearly 400 years. It makes much more sense that he might have arrived in that area as an adult as part of a much larger migration.

That migration seems to be validated by the appearance of the art of divination in Caria and Lydia during the time of Homer, which was a clear import from Cyprus, where it had been practised at least since the 14th century BC. In the clay letters of Ugarit, there are mentions of augury related to Cyprus. It seems that the arrival of the diviners in Lydia and Caria must have happened at the time of the arrival of the Ionians. So it can be deduced that the Ionians also came from Cyprus.

Many have previously argued that the Ionians were originally from Cyprus. In the Bible, one of Noah's sons was called Japheth, and one of Japheth's sons was called Javan. Isidoro of Seville believed that all Europeans descended from Japheth. It is also common belief that Javan was the Hebrew version of what Greeks called Ionians, and two out of four of Javans children are associated with Cyprus. Javan's sons, Elishah and Kittim, are believed to be places in Cyprus (Alashia, Kition). Even the name of Japheth seems related to Lapith. But the most obvious proof that the Cypriots were the original Ionians comes from architecture. What in Greek temple-building terms is called Ionian style actually appears to have originated in Cyprus. Ionian style that was used in Ionia from the 6th century BC was used in Cyprus and the east almost two centuries earlier.

We also have very clear Cypriot evidence from the names of places. Cities appear all over Greece and Anatolia with the same names as ones in Cyprus. Chytri, Cnidos, and Erythrea are places in Ionia that have much older counterparts in Cyprus. We also see a city called Aphrodisia named after Aphrodite and one called Iassus after a ruling dynasty in Cyprus.

If the Ionians arrived from Cyprus, it is also obvious that their writers would have followed the same path. That Homer was not from Ionia seems to be confirmed by the fact that the language he used was not Ionian Greek. Probably from the travels he undertook he created his own language, which is now called Homeric Greek.

The travels from Cyprus to Anatolia are also clearly explained by events of the time. During the Assyrian invasion of Cyprus (in the reign of King Sargon II 721–705 BC), many Cypriots would have fled the invading hordes and sought refuge in Asia Minor and Greece. This move seems to coincide with the arrival of script to Greece.

In the context of the Assyrian invasion of Cyprus, the origin of the name Homer seems to make a lot more sense than in Greece. Homer is a Greek name attested in Aeolic-speaking areas on the western coast of Anatolia. Lucian, in his True History, describes him as a Babylonian called Tigranes, who assumed the name Homer when taken 'hostage' (homeros) by the Greeks. Lucian was not a historian but a satirist of Assyrian origin.

If instead of being a Babylonian taken hostage by the Greeks, he was a Greek taken hostage by the Babylonians (Assyrians), the story seems to get more believable. A Babylonian taken hostage by Greeks seems to contradict all the historical facts of the time. As Pausanias writes:

'The inhabitants of Ios still show the tomb of Homer, and in another part of the island the tomb of Clymene, who they say was Homer's mother. But the people of Cyprus, for they too claim Homer as their own, and say that Themisto (one of the women of their country) was his mother, cite the following prophetical verses of Euclus touching Homer's birth;

In sea-girt Cyprus shall a great poet one day be born, whom divine Themisto shall give birth to in the country, a poet whose fame shall spread far from wealthy Salamis. And he leaving Cyprus and sailing over the sea shall first sing the woes of spacious Hellas, and shall all his days be immortal and ever fresh.'

Pausanias ends his reference about the birth of Homer in Cyprus with the following words:

'These things I have heard and I have read the oracles, but express no private opinion about either the age or date of Homer.'

To Pausanias, the Cypriot birth of Homer was not in doubt. The only doubt to him was the date or age of Homer. His birth being somewhere around Salamis and his death in the island of Ios were apparently established facts.

It is not just from Pausanias that we can deduce that Homer was from the area of Salamis. Other legends about Homer seem to confirm a link with the island of Cyprus. He was believed to have been the author of another epic called *Cypria*, supposedly a prologue to the *Iliad*. It contained an account of the judgement of Paris, the rape of Helena, the abandonment of Philoctetes on the island of Lemnos, the landing of the Achaeans on the coast of Asia Minor, and the first engagement before Troy. It is also believed that the 'Trojan Battle order' from the *Iliad* was taken from the *Cypria*. This book was later attributed to Stasinus of Cyprus, but legend again makes clear that it was Homer who wrote the *Cypria* on the occasion of his daughter's wedding to Stasinus. If Homer's daughter married a Cypriot and his mother was also a Cypriot, it seems that the whole family must have lived in Cyprus. If, after being held hostage, he fled to the safety of Lydian-controlled Halicarnassus, that would explain the fact that Homeric script was also related to western Anatolia. Further, an inscription found in 1995 at Halicarnassus names the poet of the Iliad as 'Kyprias', possibly referring to the author's origin.

The dialect of the Greek language spoken in Cyprus at the time is called Arcado-cypriot, due to the similarities of the Arcadian language with the Cypriot language. In a 1926 article called 'Homeric Words in Arcadian Inscriptions', C.M. Bowra writes:

'it has been known for many years that inscriptions in the Arcadian dialect contain a considerable number of words which occur commonly in the Homeric poems and rarely, if at all, elsewhere.'[153]

This statement is difficult to comprehend if Homer was from Anatolia, as there was no relation between the language of Arcadia and the language of Halicarnassus. If you consider the possibility that Homer was from Cyprus, however, it makes perfect sense that he would have used the Arcado-Cypriot language.

There is another possible explanation to the fact that Halicarnassus claims Homer as a local. The link would mean a royal connection between Homer and Lydia (where Halicarnassus was situated). The Lydians claim descent from Heracles through his marriage to Queen Omphale.

In 'Of the origin of Homer and Hesiod and of their Contest' one reads:

'Homer himself was called Meles or, according to different accounts, Melesigenes or Altes. Some authorities say he was called Homer, because his father was given as a hostage to the Persians by the men of Cyprus.'[54]

It all seems to fit. The father of Homer being given as a hostage to the Persians by the Cypriots. Not any hostage, but probably a king or prince of one of the Cypriot kingdoms—Salamis, if we believe the ancient writers. His son migrated to the safety of Lydia. Once there he was made king. In historic records we have a king of Lydia called Meles between 745 and 733 BC, a member of the Heraclid family. His son, Candaules, became the last ruler of the Heraclid dynasty when Meles was murdered by Gyges. Meles II, according to Nicolaus of Damascus went into exile in Babylon. Candaules's son was sent to Cappadocia as a hostage—both being reasonable explanations for the name he was given. Homer being the king of the Lydians would explain the construction of a temple dedicated to him. It also makes sense, as only the elite of any areas would know how to write. It seems that Homer might have been the son of a king of Salamis and became king of Lydia himself when they were forced to leave Cyprus.

If Homer was, as ancient writers state, a Cypriot, we must view his version of the Trojan conflict through an entirely different lens. The figures given in the catalogue of ships might have been the exact numbers of combatants sent to war and the numbers of how many ships, their leaders and number of troops written down and being passed through generations of Cypriots in their Cypriot language until Homer wrote The Iliad.

Chapter 5
ATLANTEAN ARMY

When Plato talks about the people of Atlantis, he is describing a major maritime empire. He also tells us that it was the Atlanteans who started the major conflict that laid waste to the ancient world. That seems to accord exactly with the Egyptian sources, which talk about a confederation of nine different types of Sea People that would bring an end to the Bronze Age. The attack of that confederation seems so similar to what Plato was describing that it cannot be a coincidence.

In the Greek world we also have the stories of the war that was responsible for the end of the Bronze Age. They tell the story of a war that resulted in major loss of life, and ended major civilizations: The Trojan War. The troops that arrived with Achilles and Agamemnon started the conflict and were believed to have incorporated a massive naval force.

Plato described Atlantis as a civilization with a formidable army. If each allotment had to provide a sixth of a chariot with two charioteers plus another two horses and spare charioteers, two hoplites, two archers, two slingers, three light-armed slingers and three javelin men, as described in Plato's account of the contributions from each of the 60,000 allotments you would get:

Chariots	10,000 with two horses
Reserve horses	20,000
Charioteers	20,000
Other chariot crew	20,000
Hoplites	120,000
Archers	120,000
Slingers	120,000
Light-armed slingers	180,000
Javelin men	180,000
Sailors	240,000
Total men	**1,000,000**

It is difficult today to understand how big such an army was, unless we have something to compare it with. Thanks to the numerous records that we have regarding the Battle of Kadesh, fought a few years prior, in 1274 BC, we can put the size of the army into perspective. Kadesh has been called the biggest chariot battle in history. In that battle, the Egyptians are believed to have had 2,000 chariots and the

Hittites about 3,700. The Atlantis chariots, with their corresponding horses and men, were nearly double the size of both these armies put together.

If we combine Egyptian and Hitite armies in the battle of Kadesh, it amounts to 100,000 combatants. This makes the Atlantean army ten times bigger than both of them together. Such an army would be the biggest army ever assembled in antiquity. The second biggest would be nearly 1,000 years later by Chandragupta Maurya (340–298 BC) who took an army of more than 700,000 people to beat the descendants of Alexander the Great.

The Atlantean navy was even more impressive, with 240,000 sailors who manned 1,200 ships. A navy of that size would have been unheard of—that is, unless you read Homer's portrayal of the Battle of Troy. In chapter 2 of the Iliad, when he lists the forces assembled to fight the Trojans, he gives a detailed list of all the allies and the number of ships sent by each one of them. If you add them all together it gives you a total of 1,186 ships.

This, of course, is not a coincidence. The possibility of these armies being the same, but just explained in a different way, has already been argued by Professor Eberhard Zangger:

> *'When summarizing these conclusions, I remembered that earthquakes, floods, and the demise of a brilliant culture are also mentioned in Plato's dialogues Timaeus and Critias. When I turned to reread these, I noticed that the philosopher's story may well represent yet another account—thus far unrecognized—of the events of the crisis years. Plato describes two prehistoric civilizations that possessed bronze weapons, chariots and writing, and he describe how a devastating war broke out between them. Those facts, and numerous additional elements of the account, have much in common with the Trojan War: Plato mentions a navy of 1200 ships; Homer, adding up the vessels of the united*

Greek army, reached a total of 1186 ships. Both Plato and Homer described the opposing armies as consisting of many allies.'

It is now reasonable to believe that the armies of the 'Greeks' in the Trojan War, the Sea People in the attacks on Egypt and elsewhere, and the Atlantean military described by Plato are all the same thing. So, why do we think that the Mycaeneans were the strongest Aegean rulers of that time?

The Role of Agamemnon?

This is probably one of the biggest misunderstandings in history. The whole story of the Mycenaean's power is based on one account, the Iliad of Homer. In that book, all the Greek troops followed Agamemnon, king of Mycenae. From the texts people understood that, without his support, it would be impossible to go to war. From there it has been assumed that the Mycenaeans were the superpower of the Mediterranean.

When Menelaus asked Agamemnon and all the other leaders to fight with him against the Trojans he was probably just invoking the law inscribed on the Pillar of Orichalcum in Atlantis:

> 'They were not to take up arms against one another, and they were all to come to the rescue if anyone in any of their cities attempted to overthrow the royal house.'

Asking Agamemnon for support on military matters was crucial, because Agamemnon was the king representing the god of war, Ares. People have wondered why such a powerful king was always represented as volatile, bloodthirsty, violent and arrogant. The answer seems clear. They are the same personality traits as those displayed by Ares. Again, this is not a coincidence.

Mythology seems to confirm the connection. The myth of how Ares killed Adonis tells that he did it disguised as a wild boar. The headgear or masks worn by the Mycenaeans leaders, were made out of wild boar tusks.

Fig. 5.1: Mycaeanean boar tusk helmet.[55]

Agamemnon was the representative of Ares, and you cannot go to battle without the support of the god of war. The headgear of the Mycenaean rulers would explain the myth of the wild boar disguise. Historians and archaeologists are now realising that Mycenaean society at this point was a violent one, more focused on war than on culture. Thus, the migration to Cyprus that followed the collapse of the Bronze Age was not even a real colonization. Maria Iacovou, Professor at the University of Cyprus in Nicosia, describes the move as follows:

> 'The Greek migration to Cyprus was a twelfth-century precolonization exodus which took place before the Ionic migration of ca 1000 BC It cannot be classified as a mother-city-and-colony type of colonization, since it took place long before the Greek polis came into existence; nor does it constitute a centre-versus-periphery case, since for the first 200–300 years of the early Iron Age, if anything it was the Greek mainland that depended on Cyprus "as source or intermediary". Indeed, the Mycenaean migration to Cyprus at the end of the Bronze Age is eloquently described as a move "from the periphery to the core, from the Provinces to Versailles". Subsequently, and until the end of the Dark Ages (ca. 900 BC), it was Cyprus that assumed the role of a cultural centre vis-a-vis a destitute Aegean world which remained on the periphery of Mediterranean contacts.'[56]

The migrations of people from politically and economic unstable areas is very common these days, but they would never be called colonizations. It would sound crazy to say that Syrians are colonizing Europe by fleeing their country's civil war. The exodus to Cyprus was clearly triggered by the instability the area suffered during the end of the Bronze Age and the stability that Cyprus offered. The violent destruction of all settlements in Greece left hardly anyone wishing to live there. In this context, the movement to Cyprus looks more like a tactical retreat to their motherland rather than colonization.

Cyprus was never in favour of war. When Menelaus and Agamemnon decided to go to war, everyone had to go with them. But once the war was over, Aphrodite could avenge the killing of Adonis by Ares.

The destruction of the settlements in Mycenaean Greece is also explained in the Iliad. Zeus resolved to destroy those settlements for bringing a war he never wanted. In the *Iliad* we read:

'Rising in anger, Zeus who drives the storm clouds thundered, "Insatiable Hera! How great are the pains that Priam and Priam's sons have heaped on you that you rage on, relentless, forever bent on razing the well-built heights of Troy?".'

Zeus was very upset about the war, so Hera gave him the solution:

'And Hera the Queen, her eyes wide, answered, "Excellent! The three cities that I love best of all are Argos and Sparta, Mycenae with streets as broad as Troy's. Raze them-whenever they stir the hatred in your heart. My cities ... I will never rise in their defense, not against you—I'd never grudge your pleasure".'

The destruction of the cities in Mycenaean Greece seemed to be clearly explained. Sparta and Mycenae were the towns of Menelaus and Agamemnon and match exactly the destruction caused by the Sea People.

The Sea People: Greeks or Atlanteans?

Mythology tells us that the destruction caused in Troy (and the rest of Anatolia) was due to the Greeks. Archaeology tells us that the destruction of Troy was caused by the Sea People. Could it be that the Sea People were the Greeks?

One of the questions that has been asked is how the Sea People, without a known land, could have taken part in all the historic events since the 17th century BC in the area of Levant and Egypt until the 12th century BC. They appear in many of the Amarna letters and on temple walls in Egypt. They are even at the Battle of Kadesh helping the Hittites. They might even appear as early as 2000BC in hieroglyphs on an obelisk in Byblos. It seemed impossible for them to be always there without holding any land.

The Sea People were a group of 'tribes' that lived somewhere in the Mediterranean. The Egyptians refer to them as the *'from the midst of the sea'*, and in some texts they are described as of the *'Great Green Sea'* or *'from the isles'*.

As historian Michael Wood explains in *In Search of the Trojan War*:

> *'The term "sea" in these sources, or "Great Green", comes to mean the eastern Mediterranean as a whole. Peoples like the Aqaiwasha, the Philistines, the Sherden and the Lukka have no original connection with Syria-Palestine, or with Egypt: they are from outside their world, over seas to the north-west. Very likely the "islands" they are from are in the Aegean.'*[57]

But those Sea People had clear eastern Mediterranean influences. In the Egyptian description of the Sea People, some of them appeared to have been circumcised. Circumcision was not a common practice in the Aegean Islands. The only known people that at that time could have been circumcised were the Jews. Some of the Sea People must have been from further east. An island on the eastern Mediterranean but outside the Aegean seems to point again to Cyprus. Cyprus was later known to have a very large Jewish population, and its location is not far from the ancestral homeland of the Jews.

So could it be that the Sea People's homeland was Cyprus? This seems to have been suggested by a pharaoh during the attacks at the end of the Bronze Age. In the Amarna letter E38, the king of Alashiya replies to the pharaoh:

> *'Say to the king of Egypt, my brother: Message of the king of Alashiya, your brother. For me all goes well, and for you may all go well. For your household, your chief wives, your sons, your horses, your chariots, among your numerous troops, in your country, among your magnates, may all go very well. "Why, my brother, do you say such a thing to me: Does my brother not know this?"*

As far as I am concerned, I have done nothing of the sort. Indeed, men of Lukki, year by year, seize villages in my own country. My brother, you say to me: "Men from your country were with them."
My brother, I myself do not know that they were with them. If men from my country were (with them), send (them back) and I will act as I see fit. You yourself do not know men from my country. They would not do such a thing. But if men from my country did do this, then you yourself do as you see fit.

Now, my brother, since you have not sent back my messenger, for this tablet it is the king's brother (as messenger). Let him write. Your messengers must tell me what I am to do. Furthermore, which ancestors of yours did such a thing to my ancestors? So no, my brother, do not be concerned.'

It is clear from the text that at least some of the people attacking Egypt were believed to be from Cyprus. The Hittites also believed that the Cypriots were the aggressors. King Suppiluliuma II (1207–1178 BC) mentions:

'The ships of Alasiya met me in the sea three times for battle, and I smote them, and I seized the ships and set fire to them in the sea.' But then: 'But when I arrived on dry land(?), th enemies from Alasiya came in multitude against me for battle. I (fought) them, and (....) me (....).'[158]

According to two of the main targets of the Sea People, the Egyptians and the Hittites, the attacks were carried out by people from Cyprus. Alashiya never referred to the whole island; just to one of the kingdoms. The nine other kingdoms of the island were probably the Sea People the Alashiyan king refers to. It makes sense as in the Egyptian temples there are references to nine different groups of Sea People. Nine kingdoms; nine Sea People.

Archaeology also seems to corroborate this. On the island of Cyprus there was destruction by the Sea People, but it was more selective than in other places. All of the places destroyed in Cyprus had something in common—big defensive walls and clear Mycaenean connections. These clearly show that they were threatened by someone. Who were they protecting themselves from?

The main threat at that time could only have been the Sea People. But in Paleokastro there is a clue to solve the mystery. In the little peninsula the people of Paleokastro built only one wall and that was to separate the peninsula from the rest of the island. It also shows most of the destruction around the wall area. This is proof that the actual invasion of the site was from the mainland.

But these are not the only clues. Even in the Bible there is a reference to the Sea People being from Cyprus. Numbers 24:24 reads:

'The Sea People gather in the north,
ships from the coast of Kittim.
They bear down on Asshur, they bear down on Eber
he too shall perish for ever.'[59]

That the city of Kition was just a continuation of the town of Atlantis seems to coincide also with the Sargon stele, which refers to Kition as 'new town' as opposed to old town. The 'new town' is located on the north side of the Salt Lake but there is also a village called Kiti on the south side showing the great influence that the old city had. The Jews called it Kittim, but Plato used the Greek equivalent, Atlantis.

The Pelasgians

If Cyprus was Atlantis and the army sent by them is the one that fought Troy, why is there no mention of the Cypriots in the Iliad's

catalogue of ships?
Actually, there is. The list of the ships follows a very clear pattern. It starts with the area north of Athens in the mainland (Boetians, Mynians, Locrians, Euboeans and Athenians) then moves on to describe the different groups that went from the Peloponessus (Argos, Mycenaeans, Lacedaemonians, Arcadians, Pylos and Elis). Homer then lists the islands on the west (Echinean Islands, Zakynthos, Kefalonia and Ithaka) and locations from Crete towards the east (Crete, Rhodes, Symi, Kos and Nysiros). After that, most ethnic groups are not named. One of the few places mentioned is the land of the Lapiths. The problem is that the only Lapiths known were the ones from mythology who fought the centaurs at the wedding of Pirithous and Hippodamia. The only known location that matches, is the ancient kingdom of Lapithos in Cyprus. The sanctuary of Ayia Irini in northwest Cyprus is within the area where the kingdom of Lapithos once stood. Archaeologists unearthed what can only be described as a 'terracotta army' filled with clay statues of centaurs. The connections with the northern area of Cyprus also extend to family links. Kyrene was the name of a famous daughter of a Lapith king, and the biggest city in that area is still today called Kyrenia. It is quite possible that they were not mentioned because the writer and the readers knew exactly who they were and where they came from. It would make sense not to cite their ethnicity if the story originated in Cyprus. And as we have seen, Homer had very close links with Cyprus.

After the Symians, Homer mentions the Pelasgians, Myrmidons, Hellenes and Achaeans. These are the troops that were under the command of Achilles. The ones that came with Achilles seem to also have many links with Cyprus. It seems clear that the Achaeans are not the ones in the Peloponessus, as they would have been mentioned in the catalogue when describing the troops from that area. Was there an Achaea in Cyprus?

The truth is that we do not know. But there are many names derived from the term Achaea in Cyprus. The village of Achna is believed to be originated from the word Achaea. There is an Achna forest. There is an Achni beach. And the Achaeans were one of the Sea People mentioned by the Egyptians.

The term Hellenes would later become a term to refer to all Greeks. But at the time of the Iliad it was not like that. As Homer writes:

'Now all those who lived in Pelasgian Argos, those who peopled Alos and Alope and Trachis, and held Phthia and Hellas where women are handsome, and were called Myrmidons and Hellenes and Achaians, their fifty ships were commanded by Achilleus.'[60]

From the text it is clear that the Hellenes are the people of Hellas. But Hellas was only a village, as were all the other places mentioned by Homer. The name Hellas is not mentioned as a place in Cyprus, but it seems very likely that what the Greeks called Hellas is what the Assyrians called Alashiya or the Jews called Elishah. In 1729, Charles Rollin wrote in his book 'The ancient history of the Egyptians, Carthaginians, Assyrians, Babylonians, Medes and Persians, Macedonians, and Grecians' that:

'Elishah is the same as Ellas, as it is rendered in the Chaldee translation.'[61]

He also points towards the same origin to the term Elysian Fields. The Elysian Fields were the place where the heroes and king went to die. It was supposed to have been ruled by Cronus. If Alashiya is the site at Enkomi, as everyone suspects, the Elysian Fields should also be in that area. There should be many rich tombs of kings and heroes there.

And of course there are. The area next to Enkomi is now called Cellarka and the Royal Tombs. This is where the tomb of Barnabas, the patron Saint of Cyprus, is to be found. You also find many other tombs of elite people. The location fits with the description as it is clearly a very fertile area, just as the Elysium was supposed to be. Hesiod placed the Elysium on the Isles of the Blessed or Nisi Makaria, a name also used to describe Cyprus.

Pelasgian was a term used by the Greeks to refer to their ancestral origin. The problem with this term is that there is not a single area where such people are located. They are everywhere and nowhere. But they seem to appear in the same places as the Sea People who undertook the destruction at the end of the Bronze Age. Romanian-Canadian linguist Ernest Klein explained the name with its connection with the sea. After all, the name seems to be derived from Pelagos ('Sea') making the Pelasgian 'Sea men'. It seems very reasonable to believe that the Sea People referred to in the term Pelasgian are the same as the Sea People that caused the destruction in 1200 BC.
Once you equate them both, some 'coincidences' seem to appear. Areas believed to have links with the Sea People also have links with the Pelasgians. Names that are linked to the Sea People also appear used with the Pelasgians. Denyen, one of the Sea People groups, seem to be the same as the Danaids of the Greeks. In a lost play of Euripides, quoted by Strabo, he clearly makes the Danaids Pelasgians:

> 'Euripides, in the Archelaus, says, "Danaus, who was the father of fifty daughters, having arrived in Argos inhabited the city of Inachus, and made a law that those who had before borne the name of Pelasgiotæ throughout Greece should be called Danai."'[62]

What is clear is that they were not from Greece as they would have spoken the same language. The Pelasgians on the other side spoke a different language. The daughters of Danaus in the play The suppliants by Aeschylus clearly do not speak Greek. As recounted on the play:

> 'I cry for mercy to these Apian highlands
> (forgive, soil of Hellas, my outlandish tongue);
> And again, again I tear
> My Tyrian veil to unsightly rags.'[63]

In this section of the text, apart from the language he also mentions the fact that they were connected to the Tyrians. Tyrians would have been one of the Sea People (the Teresh) mentioned in the Egyptian texts. If the Danaids were Pelasgians, the people who lived in the city that King Pelasgos created, and named by Homer Pelasgian Argos, were obviously Danaids, and Sea People at the same time.

William E. Gladstone, the 19th-century British Prime Minister and trained classicist, wrote an in-depth analysis on the origin of the Greeks. He noted that if the Pelasgians did take part in the Trojan War, they were not all on the side of the Greeks. He believed that the people from Troy were also Pelasgians. He clearly mentions the Ionians as one of the main Pelasgian people. All those people seem to have another thing in common—they were all related to the royal line of Iasus. Since the Iasonides ruled Cyprus, it should also prove that Cyprus would have been a Pelasgian land. Gladstone wrote:

'The hypothesis, that the population of Cyprus was purely or generally Pelasgian, appears to square remarkably with the facts. For then, upon the one hand, they would naturally be disinclined to interfere on behalf of the Greeks in a war where all purely Pelasgian sympathies would (as we must for the present take for granted) incline them towards Troy.'[64]

In this context it seems clear why the leader of the troops of Pelasgian Argos, Achilles, was reluctant to take part in the war. It also explains why he never had a good relationship with Agamemnon. And it clearly explains why he helps the priestess of the temple of Apollo of Troy. This could even fit the events described by Homer. He tells how Cinyras did not want to send any help to fight at Troy. He sent the famous 50 ships made out of clay. Achilles did not want to go either. So where is the city of Pelasgian Argos in Cyprus? The answer was probably given by Ptolemy Hephaestion when he wrote:

'She found it in Argos, a town of Kypros, in the sanctuary of Apollo Erithios.'[65]

The main candidate to be the city called Argos is Kourion. We know that Kourion is only an epithet. We also know that the city was, according to mythology, founded by the Argives. What other name would Argives give their new city but Argos?

When that is accepted, the devotion that Achilles had for the god Apollo becomes clear. It also becomes obvious why Achilles is always shown as a young beardless youth—a Kouros. A Kouros from Kourion. In other words, Achilles was a Cypriot.

If Achilles was from Kourion, is there any evidence linking him to the town? The Romans appear to have believed he had a relationship with Kourion. They actually had a house marked with a beautiful mosaic of Achilles inside. It could well be that they were just making a mark to remember the house of the Greek hero. In the archaeological site of Kourion, they still today call the site of the mosaic the house of Achilles.

In the Iliad, when Achilles was to fight Hector he takes the helmet that the husband of the Cypriot goddess made for him,

'and tossed his bright four-horned helm; and fair about it waved the plumes wrought of gold, that Hephaestus had set thick about the crest.'[66]

Horned helmets are also present in the Egyptian descriptions of the Sea People, and they are the same as those of the horned gods of Cyprus. No wonder they called Cyprus Kerastia, meaning land of the horns.

The fact that the troops with Achilles were the best-armed and best fighters seems to fit the fact that they came from a land where the metal to create those weapons and armours was produced. The fact that Achilles's mother had his arms and armour made by Hephaestus would also fit the theory. It makes sense that the fighter with the best armour comes from the land of metalwork. It all seems to agree with Hesiod's account of Achilles's greaves being made of orichalcum: 'He spoke thus and placed around his legs greaves of shining mountain-bronze,[67] the famous gift of Hephaestus.'[68]

Achilles was a Cypriot using Cypriot metals for his shield and greaves and helmets. But other gods besides Apollo had Pelasgian sympathies. Gladstone recounts:

'There is another sign, which strongly tends to connect Cyprus with the Pelasgian races, especially those which belong to Asia. It is the worship of Venus, who had in that island her special sanctuary, and who, upon her detection in the Odyssey takes refuge there.... We must consider her as a peculiarly, and perhaps in Homer's time almost Pelasgian deity; and her local abode at Paphos may be taken as a marked sign, accordingly, of the Pelasgianism of Cyprus.'[69]

It we take Cyprus as the original home of the Pelasgians, the idea that the Greeks came from those people seems to accord with archaeological evidence, linguistic analysis, and DNA results discussed in Chapter 1. And if the Cypriots were Pelasgians, it strongly suggests that they also were the Sea People. After all, the translation of Pelasgian is People of the Sea.

The three terms Atlantean, Pelasgians, and Sea People refer to a seafaring society. Atlantis and Pelasgian are both terms also used to explain the foreign origin of Greece. But at the end they all seem to point to the same place: Cyprus.

Aeschylus already suggested the Cypriot origin of the Greeks in the play Seven against Thebes

'You too, Cyprian goddess, mother of our race'[70]

Chapter 6
THE LEGACY OF ATLANTIS

In the previous chapters, we have seen all the ways in which Cyprus matches the ancient descriptions of the island of Atlantis. Cyprus and Atlantis shared the same geography and political systems. An ancient harbour city matching the precise measurements from Plato can be found in Cyprus, with canals and the remains of its boats. The islands shared the same religion and featured prominent temples. We even have the trident of Poseidon, the god of Atlantis, found in the centre of the ancient capital.

Yet if Atlantis did exist, why were there no indications of this extremely powerful empire in the Mediterranean Sea? Ancient written records should acknowledge this powerful empire and its mighty rulers.
In truth, the evidence was there all along.

We have already seen that the Hebrew texts used to call all the Mediterranean Sea and its coastal areas the lands of Kittim as a unity. We also know that all the trade undertaken from any of the islands was always done through Cyprus.
All the correspondence between the Cypriots and other lands shows levels of respect that would only make sense if Cyprus was

one of the superpowers of the time. The respect that the pharaohs and Cypriot rulers show for each other seems to indicate that they were on an equal level. Anyone researching the diplomatic texts from the Bronze Age will agree that there was a very clear protocol when addressing the pharaoh. And there are mainly three ways to address him. The first would apply to the countries that are under the control of the Egyptians. Some independent countries also would address the pharaoh this way to denote a complete subordination and acknowledging Egyptian might. Around 1347 BC, King Abi-Milku from Tyre sent a letter to Pharaoh Amenhotep III:

'To the king, my lord, my god, my Sun: Message of Abi-Milku, your servant. I fall at the feet of the king, my lord, 7 times and 7 times. I am the dirt under the sandals of the king, my lord. My lord is the Sun who comes forth over all lands day by day, according to the way (of being) the sun, his gracious father, who gives life by his sweet breath and returns with his north wind; who establishes the entire land in peace, by the power of his arm : ha-ap-si; who gives forth his cry in the sky like Baal, and all the land is frightened at his cry.'[71]

During the time of the Amarna letters, people addressing the pharaoh in this way included King Abdu-Heba of Jerusalem and King Aziru of Amurru in modern-day Lebanon. Most of the land between Egypt and modern-day Lebanon addressed the pharaoh in a very similar manner to Abi-Milku. They also made clear that they were 'the dirt under Pharaoh's sandals' by bowing seven times.

Other kingdoms that did not feel inferior to Egypt showed their equality by referring to the pharaohs as 'my brother', as in this letter sent by the Babylonian king Burra-Buriyaš II to Amenhotep IV:

'Say to Naphurureya, king of Egypt, my brother Thus Burra-Buriyaš Great king the king of Karaduniyaš your brother. For me and my household and my horses and my chariots and my magnates and

my country all goes very well For my brother and his household and his horses and his chariots and his magnated and his country may all go very well'[172]

Other kingdoms that addressed the pharaoh in this manner included Mitanni in northern Syria, where King Tushratta had his sister and his daughter married to the pharaoh. The king of the Hittites also sent letters to the pharaohs in very familiar terms:

'The messages I sent to your father (Amenhotep III) and the wishes he expressed to me will certainly be renewed between us. O King, I did not reject anything your father asked for, and your father never neglected none of the wishes I expressed, but granted me everything. Why have you, my brother, refused to send me what your father during his lifetime has sent me?
Now, my brother, you have acceded to the throne of your father, and similarly as your father and I have sent each other gifts of friendship, I wish good friendship to exist between you and me. I have expressed a wish to your father..'[173]

The king of Alashiya in Cyprus also addressed the pharaoh in this manner:

'S(ay to the K)ing of Egypt, my brother. (message) of the king of Alashiya, your brother: For me all goes well. For my household, my wifes, my sons, my magnates, my horses, my chariots, and in my country, all goes very well. For my brother may all go well. For your household, your wives, your sons, your magnates, your horses, your chariots, and in your country, may all go very well. My brother, I herewith send my messenger with your messenger to Egypt. I herewith sendto you 500 (?) of copper; As my brother's greeting-gift I send to you. My brother, do not be concerned that the amount of copper is small. Behold, the hand of Nergal is now in my country, he has slainall th men of my country, and there is not a (single) copper-worker.'[174]

It seems clear that in diplomatic terms, Alashiya was at least at the same level as Egyptians, Hittites and Babylonians. Basically they were from the group of superpowers of the time.

The king of Alashiya had correspondence with other lands. From the letters from Ugarit, you see another type of address:

> *'Say to the king of Alashiya, my father: Thus says (your) son Niqmaddu (king of Ugarit), your son: (I fall at) the feet of my father. May my father be (well)! May your palaces, (your) wives, (your) infantry, your) chariots, (your) horses, and everything that belongs to the king of Alashiya, (my father), be very, very well!'*[75]

The king of Ugarit calls the king of Alashiya 'my father' and falls at his feet in a clear sign of subordination, similar to the one shown by the lands of Canaan to the pharaoh.

The Mycenaeans do not appear in any of these letters or tablets, and it seems that all their trading relations with the Egyptians went through the Cypriot kings. Thus, it seems clear that Cyprus was far more respected in the Bronze Age than today.

The importance of Cyprus in antiquity was still known during the Middle Ages. Eusebios of Caesarea wrote that Cyprus was one of the countries that ruled the seas after the Trojan War, along with Pelasgians, Lydians, Thracians, Rhodians, Phrygians and Phoenicians. All of those areas used to belong to the ancient empire of Atlantis.
Yet somehow, because the myths passed down rarely identify Cyprus by name, its importance has faded in favour of societies like Mesopotamia, Egypt and the Levant. But if you look closely at the myths passed down from each, you can see similarities that may point to a common source.

The Island of Death and Life

According to the mythology of those cultures, it was the gods who gave us civilization, and those gods were believed to live on an island. According to the Mesopotamian myths, the island of Dilmun was the centre of civilization. Accounts of Dilmun in some ways resemble the Garden of Eden. To reach Dilmun, it was necessary to travel through the land of the cedars (modern-day Lebanon) and then take the ferry across to the island. Similarly, the Egyptians said that one must travel by boat to reach the island of the gods, which was located just past the Nile delta. Following these directions, Cyprus is the only island that makes sense as a destination north of Egypt or east of Mesopotamia.

Myths in all these areas feature the character of the ferryman. A character that illustrates the relation of humans to gods in the different civilizations.

In ancient Egypt, the pharaohs were buried in the pyramids. Enclosed in those edifices, they awaited their entrance into the afterlife. For them, the afterlife was something very real. After death, they went through a long preparation process. Most significant was the requirement for a body in which to inhabit their new existence in the afterlife. That was arranged with the mummification of the corpse, a complex process that clearly preserved the body for many years. Each mummy was buried with vast amounts of treasure, everyday items, pets, food and even slaves to prepare for the long journey into the afterlife.

Egyptians believed that they had to cross a big body of water, which is why solar boats or barges were buried next to pyramids. The boats were made from a wood not native to Egypt but abundant in Lebanon and Cyprus: the cedar. In earlier times, before the boats were constructed out of cedar, they were made out of papyrus, as attested to in the Book of the Dead. Some of the solar boats found show signs of actually having been used in water. The boat was a necessary means to reach heaven and, because of that, myths always mention the boats and people who helped the pharaoh to make the journey.

Aken was the patron of Mahaf, the ferryman, who would take the pharoahs into the afterlife on a boat named Meseket. Aken would ask Mahaf to deliver the pharaohs to heaven. In later myths the name of the ferryman changed to Cherti, a name that bears a resemblance to the Greek Charon.
The description of the trip to the underworld began in a place very similar to the world they were used to living in, with the same features of real life in Egypt. The trip started in an underworld called Duat, where the heart of the pharaoh would be weighed. If the heart weighed the same as a feather, then the dead could begin the journey. It was a long and dangerous journey by boat into Aaru, the heaven of Egyptian mythology where Isis and Osiris ruled. Heaven was always represented as an island. And on that island was where you would find all the gods.

In 1954 Carleton Stevens Coon, American physical anthropologist, Professor of Anthropology at the University of Pennsylvania, Lecturer and Professor at Harvard, and President of the American Association of Physical Anthropologists, wrote The Story of Man. In it, talking about Aaru, he wrote:

'Osiris's home was not in the west, as is usual with such happy hunting grounds, but in the north. The land was foggy and bordered with high mountains, some of which were volcanic. On the side away from the mountains stood a huge lake, and in between lay a network of rivers and irrigation ditches. Toward the mountains rose a dense forest, while away from them and away

from the tillage stretched a desert. Many of the trees were conifers, sacred to Osiris. In a hall built of reeds lived the lord of the after world.[176]

This is certainly not an Egyptian landscape. But looking at the description of that place, you will find certain similarities with Cyprus. It was a land that had high mountains with lakes on the opposite side from the mountains and was full of conifers. Doctor Coon placed that island in the north of Egypt, and the only island to the north of Egypt is Cyprus. The description seems to fit not only the land of the Egyptian gods but also Plato's description of Atlantis, with its round-structured harbour, lake and canals.

An island identical to the Elysian Fields of the Greeks was described in the Book of the Dead. In a chapter found on the Papyrus of Nebseni from the 18th dynasty of Egypt, there is a map showing how to get there. Looking at the island located at the bottom left of the map, you can clearly recognize (although reversed) the lamb-chop shape associated with the island of Cyprus.

Fig. 6.1: The Elysian Fields of the Egyptians according to the Papyrus of Nebseni [77]

Babylonian mythology also records the figure of the ferryman. There, he was called Urshanabi. The Epic of Gilgamesh tells the story of Gilgamesh, king of Uruk, a kingdom located by the river Euphrates, some 30 kilometres east of modern As-Samawah, Iraq. From Uruk, Gilgamesh embarks on a journey that takes him to the cedar forests, a place clearly located in modern-day Lebanon. He then crosses the tunnel of Mount Mashu, which is usually identified with the whole of the parallel Lebanon and Anti-Lebanon ranges, with the narrow gap between these mountains constituting the tunnel. After killing a monster, he builds a raft out of cedar trees. Urshanabi then steers the raft to Dilmun, *'the land of the living'*.

Dilmun was considered the origin of the Garden of Eden, where the descendants of the survivors of the flood lived. Exactly as Cyprus was, where Kittim, the great-grandson of Noah lived.

In Mesopotamian texts, Dilmun is also mentioned as a source of copper. In an Akkadian text found in Babylon, Dilmun and Alashiya are mentioned together. This suggests that they were around the same place, and we know that Alashiya was a place in Cyprus:

> '(And) twelve minas of refined Alashiyan and Dimunite copper.'[78]

The first inscription referring to Dilmun is from the reign of King Ur-Nanshe of Lagash (c. 2300 BC) found in a door socket:

> 'The ships of Dilmun brought him wood as tribute from foreign lands.'[79]

Some researchers have identified Bahrain as Dilmun. But Bahrain does not match any of the descriptions of the Garden of Eden. You would not have to pass the land of the cedars to reach it, nor was it a major supplier of wood. Bahrain also did not have any of the descendants of the flood living on it. Cyprus, on the other hand, has always been linked to the descendants of the flood. Cyprus is the only island which would fit the description as a source of copper with Eden-like weather and vegetation, and one had to cross the land of the cedars to reach.

The Greek myth is slightly different. In Greek mythology the ferryman is called Charon. But the ferryman of the Greek world goes the other way round, completely the opposite from his Egyptian and Babylonian counterpart. Charon the ferryman did not take people to heaven; he took them to the underworld. When people died in the Greek world they used to put a coin, normally an obol or a drachma, on the eyes of the deceased to pay for Charon's fees to reach the land of Hades. He travelled from the land of the living to the land of the dead.

It seems that the three mythologies were referring to the same place. That is why the Greek world travels from the island to the underworld and the Mesopotamians and Egyptians travel from their lands to the island of the gods.

The Egyptians going north and the Mesopotamians going past Phoenicia means that the island can only be Cyprus. If the Greek gods originated in Cyprus, it is reasonable to believe that their myths did too.

Until now it has been believed that the myths of Egypt and Mesopotamia influenced Greek culture. But, if you believe Plato and genetic analysis, Cypriot myths might have influenced all the countries around them.

Could it be that the myths of Adonis and Aphrodite from Cypriot mythology were the origin of the Egyptian and Babylonian myths? If you look at the mythology of many cultures, the story of Aphrodite and Adonis and his death and resurrection seems to be present everywhere.

The Babylonians had the stories of Ishtar or Inanna and Tammuz. Tammuz was a shepherd-hunter who died a violent death. Ishtar mourns his death and he eventually resurrects. Since then, the worship of the god occurs on Ishtar week. Christians now call it Easter week. In Anatolia, the same story is told with Attis and Cybele. Attis is the god who dies and resurrects, and Cybele the mother figure who mourns his death. The Phoenicians had exactly the same story with Astarte and Adonai. Adonai was the god who would die and resurrect. The Egyptians had the same story but told with different names. Isis is the goddess that would mourn the death of her lover Osiris, just like the Paphian goddess. He would become the god of death and resurrection, just like Adonis.

It seems clear that all these stories refer to the same Gods. The male character was death and resurrection, and the female was the representation of Venus. But these are not the only similarities. All the female characters appear in many different cultures as having wings. Ishtar and Inanna are clearly shown as having wings. Isis is also represented as having wings. While the Cypriot goddess is not usually represented with wings, it is clear that she had some wings in her genes, as her son Eros clearly had them.

The Phoenician term Adonai was only an epithet that meant 'Our Lord'. In Egypt the use of Osiris could probably be derived from the Cypriot 'O Kirios' which meant 'Our Lord'. In the 9th century, George Choiroboskos wrote about the origin of words:

'Kiris: this is a kind of falcon. But among the Cypriots Adonis is called Kiris.' [80]

If the Cypriots called Adonis 'O Kiris' it would explain why the Egyptians would use that name too. It also explains why Horus, the representation of the resurrected Osiris or the son of Isis, is always represented as a man with the head of a falcon. Horus and Eros were both creatures with feathers.

Isis = Iasus (Cypriot ruling dynasty according to Homer), the Goddess

Osiris = O Kirios (Adonis)

Horus = Eros

All the representations seem to depict those early uses of animal parts as masks or dresses and all seem to tell the old Paphian story. It is therefore no surprise that when a new cult of a sect appeared within the Jewish world, they would tell exactly the same story, where a man would die and resurrect and his partner would be a woman of ill repute. They even took the young winged creatures and called them angels. But the story is still the same.

The Atlantean Diaspora

In ancient times, they used to mark what they believed was the centre of the Earth with what they called 'the Omphalos', which translates as 'navel', believed to be the navel of the Earth 'Omphalos tis Gis'. In the Middle Ages it was believed that the centre was in Jerusalem's Church of the Holy Sepulchre. Before that, in Istanbul they called the spot where they crowned the kings inside the church of Hagia Sophia the Omphalion, believing that this was the centre of the Earth. Much earlier the Greeks believed that the Omphalos was in Delphi. But the earliest location for the Omphalos was in Cyprus, in the temple of Aphrodite. Still today you can see the stone that, according to myth, Rhea wrapped in cloth and gave to Cronus, who wanted to eat his son Zeus.

Located inside the museum of Kouklia, it was believed also to be a representation of Aphrodite or Mother Earth.[81] That the centre of the earth was within the Mediterranean, was clear to both Greeks and Romans. The Greeks call the sea Mesogios, which translates 'centre of the earth'. The Romans called it Mediterraneum, but the meaning was still the same. The centre of the earth and the navel at its centre. In an early medieval text called Historiae or Chiliades, we read:

> *'In ancient times the power of Cyprus extended thus far and beyond.'*[82]

So what happened? Why do we not remember Cyprus as one of the great ancient civilizations like Mesopotamia, Egypt, Greece or Rome? With the tsunami that engulfed the island around 1200 BC, many people would have died in Cyprus. That is the reason the island was able to accept so many migrants from war-ridden Greece. The destruction of all the coastal cities is also the reason why mythology says that the fighters from the Trojan War had to build new cities when they arrived. In the case of the Salt Lake in Larnaka, they built Kition next to it.

But as Plato said, there were countless people in the mountains, and those were the people that survived the flood. If you look in the phone book in Cyprus, you can still find the names of the gods and heroes in people's surnames: Heracleus, Iasonides, Perseas are some of the heroes' names that have been carried through time. Demetriou, Kyprianou, Dionysiou, Athienitis echo the names of the gods.

We also know that during the 9th and 8th centuries BC, quite a few of them moved to Greece. The first settlements in Greece after the Dark Ages seem to have considerable influence from Cyprus. In Euboea, one of the first areas developed after the Dark Ages, the tombs unearthed are full of Cypriot goods. We also know that the language spoken in Arcadia was very similar to Cypriot. We have seen that the orientalisation of Greece took place during the years when Cyprus was threatened by the Assyrians (Giants). We also know that the people in Greece ever since called themselves the people of Hellas (Alashiya).

It is clear that the Greeks and Cypriots are descendants of the people of Atlantis. But some of the other descendants of Atlantis may not be so obvious.

Macedonian Atlanteans

The area between ancient Greece and the land of the Thracians was occupied by what was called the kingdom of Macedon. The land stretched from the western coast in the area of Dodona, near the Adriatic Sea, across to the eastern coast and the peninsula of Athos near Thessaloniki.

Rulers of this land always claimed Argian origin. The most famous rulers of this dynasty were Philip II and his son Alexander III, also known as Alexander the Great.

It seems that the genealogy of the Macedonians was well known right up until the Middle Ages. In the Chronicon, George Hamartologos wrote that 'Macedonians were once called Kitians.' This seems to point towards the idea that the ancient city of Argos where the Macedonian kings were supposed to come from was the one in Cyprus and not the one in Greece.

The Macedonians being of Cypriot origin would certainly explain why Alexander the Great encountered fierce resistance during his campaign to conquer the Peloponnesus, where the Greek Argos was. He also had to fight to conquer the area around Amphipolis and Thrace. All the areas that he fought to conquer are very well documented. All except Cyprus. It seemed that Alexander never had to conquer Cyprus. It was as though Cyprus was always on his side.

It could well be that Alexander was a descendant of a Cypriot family. Epiphanios of Salamis seems to confirm that in the 4th century AD when he wrote in Adversus Haereses or Panarion:

'Now anyone can see that Citium means the island of Cyprus, for Citians are Cypriotes and Rhodians. Moreover, the Cypriote and Rhodian stock had settled in Macedonia; thus Alexander of Macedon was Citian. And this is why the (first) Book of the Maccabees (1.1) says, "He (Alexander the Great) came out of the land of the Citians.'[83]

From this text we clearly see that some people in Salamis also believed that Alexander came from the area around Cition. It is also well attested that when going into battle his weapon of choice was his Citian sword.

But confirmation seems to come directly from his mother, Olympias, who always claimed that Alexander was not the son of Philip but the son of Zeus. Once you realize that Mount Olympus, home of Zeus and his temple, was the mountain of Stavrovouni, the closest mountain to the town of Cition, everything makes sense. Even Alexander himself liked to be called the 'Son of Zeus'. The oracle of Didyma also confirmed that Alexander was the son of Zeus. From Hyperides:

'But when the Areopagus postponed its statement on the grounds that it had not yet discovered the truth, you conceded in the Assembly that Alexander might be the son of Zeus and Poseidon too if he wished.'[184]

Alexander the Great was half Cypriot. The whole of Macedonia and northern Greece was of Cypriot descent.

Phoenician Atlanteans

The Phoenicians were sea people—just as the people from Atlantis were.

But the Phoenicians' descent from Cyprus is a slightly more complicated situation. We know from texts that Phoencians were around well before the collapse of the Bronze Age. We also know that the cities in what later would be called Phoenicia had existed since at least 3200 BC. But there is a point in history when the evolution of these people changed dramatically. That is at the end of the Bronze Age, when the city of Atlantis was flooded. At around 1200 BC, the cities in Phoenicia seem to get a major push in their development. They start to grow very rapidly. It could well be that a large number of the people from the island of Atlantis migrated to that area.

The idea that the Cypriots and Phoenicians were related is not new.

We know from mythology that the city of Tyre is related to Poseidon. Tyro in Greek mythology was married to Poseidon, the god of Atlantis. In historical terms we have evidence that one of the most famous of Paphian kings, Pygmalion, was also the king of Tyre in the legend of the founding of Carthage.

The city of Beirut is also linked to Cyprus. According to mythology Aphrodite and Adonis had two children, Golgos and Beroe. Golgos was the city of Golgoi in Cyprus and Beroe was the nymph of Beirut. Beroe was wooed by Dionysus and Poseidon, but it was the latter who married her. The fact the Beroe was a daughter of Aphrodite and Adonis makes her of Cypriot descent. The fact that she eventually married Poseidon links her to Atlantis.

If mythology gives us a Cypriot origin of the Phoenicians, does mythology also explain the move to the area of Phoenicia?

The idea of a catastrophe occurring and the Phoenicians having to migrate to another land where they would settle and flourish also exists within myth. It is as clear as the myth of the Phoenix. The Phoenix was a bird that rose from the ashes of its predecessor. That is what seems to have happened with the Atlanteans and Phoenicians. Phoenix the Phoenician. The colour red that was associated with that bird is the colour of the bird that still lives in the area where we have located Atlantis. The flamingos of the Larnaka Salt Lake become dark pink, just like the Phoenix. The name of the flamingos is also related to the Phoenix, as their ancient name was Phoenicopterus.

If the Phoenicians were also from Atlantis or of Cypriot origin, it would certainly explain why during the Greek and Phoenician expansion around the Mediterranean there was no confrontation between them. A Cypriot origin of the Phoenicians might not even surprise some historians and archaeologists, as some have described Cyprus as 'more Phoenician than Phoenicia'.[85]

It also helps to make sense of the myth of the kidnapping of Europa. Zeus disguises himself as a bull and goes to Phoenicia to kidnap Europa and then cross the sea. Why would he disguise himself as a bull if he knew he had to cross the sea? Not the most obvious choice for swimming. If the Phoenicians were from the Salt Lake in Larnaka, however, that makes it more plausible that the kidnapping took place in Cyprus. After all, Zeus's home was just a few kilometres away on Mount Stavrovouni and a disguise as a bull will make him go unnoticed within the temple of Poseidon in Atlantis where the bulls roamed free. It would also explain why the 'Greeks' would choose a foreign alphabet to be used as their language. A Cypriot origin of the Phoenician alphabet would again make much more sense and explain why it was the chosen one.

To go even further, the names of the Phoenician and Atlantean rulers suggest a connection. The father of Europa was called Agenor 'Αγήνορας'. The ruler of the island of Atlantis was called Evenor 'Ευήνορας' by Plato. The names seem too similar to be mere coincidence. The difference might have been a simple mistake by an Egyptian priest relating to events from more than 600 years before his time.

If the Phoenicians were the people from the town of Atlg who moved to the mainland, it would also fit exactly with what Herodotus stated in the first page of Histories:

'According to learned Persians, it was the Phoenicians who caused the conflict.'

This only can be explained if the Phoenicians and the Sea People were the same. The people who Plato said started the conflict (Atlanteans), the ones who Egypt said started the war (Sea People) and the ones who Herodotus said caused the conflict (Phoenicians) were all the same people.

North African Atlanteans

The Assyrians also conquered Phoenicia. That was the reason why, at the same time the Cypriots would move west towards Greece, the Phoenicians would follow the north coast of Africa. They would colonize many places around the Mediterranean all the way to the Iberian Peninsula.

The most important colony of the Phoenicians in North Africa would be Carthage. The myth of the foundation of Carthage also shows some Cypriot influence. In the Aeneid, Virgil explains how Aeneas travelled from Troy to the land of the Polyphemus, the son of Poseidon. The same Polyphemus who was in the founding myth of Paphos with Galatea and Pygmalion. From Cyprus he travelled to Carthage. Aeneas was the son of Anchises, a warrior on the side of the Trojans, but he was not purely Trojan. His mother was Cypriot—the great goddess Aphrodite. Once he arrived in Carthage, he met Queen Dido. Dido appears as Elissa in other sources, suggesting her Alashiyan origin. She also appears as the sister of King Pygmalion.

In archaeological terms we might even have an Atlantean connection with Carthage. The construction of the ancient harbour of the city, with parts still visible today, resembles the setting of the city harbour of Atlantis: a round island surrounded by a circle of water in turn surrounded by land.

Fig. 6.2: Representation of Carthage and its harbour.[86]

The distribution is very similar. Even the harbour entrance was situated facing south, just like in Atlantis.

The Phoenicians colonized all the coast of North Africa right up to what we now call Morocco. It is no surprise that the mountain range that goes from Carthage to Morocco is called Atlas. According to Herodotus, the people who lived there were the Atlantes. In mythological terms North Africa is also related to Poseidon. Anteus was a Giant king of Libya, who was also known as Anti by the Berbers. Apollodurus names him:

'Antaios, a son of Poseidon, who compelled strangers to wrestle with him and kill them.'[87]

In Egypt we have already seen that their gods lived on an island north of the Nile delta, clearly pointing towards Cyprus. But the Egyptian connections to Cyprus did not stop there. Apollodorus explains:

'Leaving Libya, he passed through Egypt, which was then under the rule of Bousiris, son of Poseidon and Lysianassa, daughter of Epaphos.Bousiris used to sacrifice strangers on an altar of Zeus, in accordance with an oracle, for barrenness had gripped the land of Egypt for nine years, and Phrasios, a skilled diviner who had come from Cyprus, said that the barrenness would come to an end if they slaughtered a male foreigner in honour of Zeus every year.'[188]

The connection of North Africa with Poseidon and Cyprus seems clear.

Roman Atlanteans

The story of the Italians is slightly different. They are, according to myth, descendants of the combatants of the Battle of Troy. Aeneas travelled to Carthage and married Alyssa (Dido). But Zeus and Aphrodite sent a messenger to remind him of his purpose and he left towards Italy. Aeneas was on the side of the Trojans and Dido on the Greek side. If you add that to the fact that she would hate Aeneas for leaving her, you get a possible origin of the enmity between the Carthaginians and the Romans.

The foundation of Rome is dated towards the 8th century BC, which seems to coincide with the myths. When Aeneas first arrived in Rome, he was welcomed by King Latinus, but they ended up fighting. Aeneas ultimately prevailed. It could well be that the war between Rome and Carthage was just a follow up to the Trojan War. The Trojans worshipped the same gods as the Greeks, so it is no surprise that the Romans would take the same gods and change their names. The only god that they did not change the name of, though, was the main god of the Trojans and one of the Cypriot gods: Apollo.

Celtic Atlanteans

The people of France also have Cypriot connections. The term Gauls comes from the ancient Galatia. The actual term used in antiquity was Hellenogalatai to clearly mark their Greek influence. The term Galatia comes from the lover of King Pygmalion of Paphos.

The French were part of a group of people called Celts. The Celts later occupied a much wider area, but they first appear in eastern France and south Germany. Again mythology explains how the Celts and the Gauls are related and their origin. According to Appian in Illyrian wars 1.2, Polyphemus married Galatea and they had three sons. Galas founder of the Gauls and Celtus founder of the Celts. It seems clear that the people in France can retrace their Cypriot origin.

The Celts had a god called Cernunnos, which was represented with stag horns. The word Cernunnos derived from the word Keras (Greek for horn). The god appears in all Celtic areas. But the most revealing appears in the coastal French town of Montagnac. The inscription is the only one written in Greek. It reads αλλετ[ει]υος καρνονου αλ[ι]σο[ντ]εας (alleteiuos karnonou alisonteas), with the last word possibly a place name based on Alashiya. It would then not be a surprise that a town appears in the Gaul area called Alesia, a name probably derived also from the original, Alashiya.

Balkan Atlanteans

The third son of Polyphemus and Galatea was called Illyrus, founder of the Illyrians. The Illyrians would settle in the area later called the Balkans. In another version of the myth, Illyrus was the son of Cadmus and Harmonia. It is from Illyrus's sons and grandsons that all the tribes of the Balkans descend.

From their son Encheleus, the Enchelaeae. From Autarieus, the Autariates. From Dardanus, the Dardani. From Taulas, the Taulantii. From Perrhaebus, the Perrhaebi. From daughter Partho, the Partheni. From Daortho, the Daors. From Dassaro, the Dassaretae. From grandson Pannonius, the Pannonians. From greatgrandson Scordiscus, the Scordisci. From Triballus, the Triballi.

Everyone in the Balkans can trace their origin to the Cypriots Galatea and Polyphemus, or Cadmus and Harmonia. The same Cadmus and Harmonia that had her necklace displayed in Amathus according to Pausanias.[89]

Iberian Atlanteans

On the Spanish peninsula, the Iberian culture appears to probably originate in the third millennium BC. Around the 6th century BC there is a noticeable development of this culture with the arrival of Phoenicians and Greeks. From the 4th century BC we also see Carthaginean influence. The main area of settlement of the Iberians was around the river Ebro (Iber). The origin of that culture is believed to be from the east. It is probably not a coincidence that in the east we have a kingdom of Iberia, situated in the area of the southern slopes of the Caucasus Mountain in the same place where myth places the origin of the Hebrew culture. Hebrews and Iberos being pronounced so similarly might not be a coincidence.
Their languages also have many similarities. Both look as if they were derived from the Phoenician alphabet. Some scholars have seen a Greek origin in the Iberian script, and in both cases they are probably right if all three languages started in Cyprus. After all, the Iberian script is a semi-syllabic that has more in common with the Cypriot

syllabary than the Phoenician and Greek based on alphabets.

From DNA research it can be seen that the Mediterranean basin was colonized by sea very quickly. In mainland Europe it took a bit longer, except the areas that had good navigable rivers. In Spain, France, Italy and the Balkans, people quickly accepted the same gods as venerated by the Greeks and the Romans. To them it would have been clear that they were worshipping the same gods anyway.

The only society which was not believed to be of Indo-European origin in Iberia is the Basque. Their language was believed to originate prior to the development of the Indo-European language. But even in Basque society and language there are signs of an eastern origin. Similarities with Caucasian languages have been claimed, as well as some similarities with ancient Greek.

There are some other issues that seem to link the Basque with the Atlanteans. If we were to find a maritime culture within the peninsula, everyone would point towards the Basque. It is a society that lives from and towards the sea. Living from the sea in the area of the whole peninsula where the waters are most inhospitable. The Bay of Biscay is a very rough sea and would not have been a first choice as a source of food unless they already were people of the sea before they settled there.

But the most striking connection and the possible explanation of the Basque origin is within one of their myths. Wentworth Webster wrote in 1879 talking about Basque legends:

'Who, or what is the Tartaro? "Oh! you mean the man with one eye in the middle of his forehead," is the prompt and universal answer.'

The legend of the Cyclops is well known within the Basque society. It seems that if the Celts are descendants of a Cyclops too, the Basque could well be the first that brought the legends to the peninsula.

Wentworth Webster also notes that the legend of the one-eyed monster was also present in eastern Africa. He relates how:

'M. d'Abaddie relates how he heard the tale told in June, 1843, in Eastern Africa, in Lat. N. 9.2, E. Lon. 34.48, by a man who had never before quitted the country.'

It seems also to support the idea that the same Cypriot-Phoenicians who colonized the area of North Africa and probably the Basque country would have taken with them one of their best-known myths. The theory that the Basque people were in the Iberian Peninsula before the arrival of the Neolithic took a heavy blow when an article in PNAS called 'Ancient genomes link early farmers from Atapuerca in Spain to modern-day Basques', showing that DNA pointed towards a common origin of Basque and the other European farmer groups. The language was different, but their DNA was the same as that of other groups that migrated from the Middle East.[90]

Germanic Atlanteans

We have already explained how from Cyprus the whole of the Mediterranean Sea was colonized. It is now worth concentrating on the northern countries of Europe.

This colonization did not come from the sea but through rivers. From figure 1.2 we can see that the development of central Europe must have come through the Danube River as the area around it seems to have been developed first. We know that the Hallstatt culture developed in central Europe since the arrival of the Neolithic. We know that the Neolithic arrived in Hungary around 6000 BC and the Tisza culture developed around 5000 BC.

In Germany, the Neolithic arrived around 5000 BC. By the year 4000

BC, it had reached Denmark, and with that the ancient sea travellers arrived back in their natural environment, where they settled down. These same people would later become what are now known as Vikings.

As we know, the Vikings were the ultimate sea people of the early Middle Ages. But the term Viking is not how they referred to themselves. Viking is a term to describe the raids they made. The actual people were the Dans. This might be showing that they were descendants of Danaus. The river they used to arrive at their destination is also known by the name Danube or Donau in the original Germanic. If you look at the Vikings, they seem very similar to the original Sea People. They used a very long narrow boat, well known for its speed and constructed with a keel and sails and rows of oars. They used round shields just like the Sea People. Even today when we think of Vikings we think of people who wore horned helmets, which have never been found within the Vikings. But deep down we seem to link them to a group of people that wore such helmets, like the Sea People did.

Viking society also resembled ancient Cypriot society, with a slave group, a freemen group, and a nobility resembling the Greek aristocracy. Within the Viking aristocracy there was a kind of democracy. They had an assembly where they would elect their rulers and decide on important issues in their communities. That is exactly what the Greek assembly, or Ekklesia, did.

But even more remarkable are the similarities with their gods. Zeus, the god of thunder and chief of all gods, became Thor. Zeus was married to Hera, a goddess related to Mother Earth. Thor was married to Sif, a goddess related to Mother Earth. Both Sif and Hera were the goddesses of marriage.

The god Wodinaz was the origin of two variants of Nordic Germanic gods: Odin and Woden. Odin had the same characteristics as Hermes and his Roman equivalent Mercury. Odin is often represented with a feathered helmet just like Hermes. Both Odin and Hermes are related to prophecy. Odin, on the other side, is a little more complex, as he actually incorporates many subjects of some of the Greek gods and myths. Odin is often depicted as with one eye, just as Polyphemus. He is also depicted as killing a dragon, as did Apollo.

The god of war of the Greeks, Ares, and the Roman Mars, are also in the Viking pantheon. The god Tyr was the Nordic god of war, often represented in the Runic language with an arrow pointing up. Ares and Mars were represented with an arrow pointing up coming out of a circle.

Freyia was the goddess of love, sex, beauty and war, similar to Aphrodite. In his book Germania, Tacitus talks about an Isis of the Suebi. This Isis was, as we have also seen earlier, a representation of the goddess Aphrodite. The connection between the Germanic and Viking gods and the eastern Mediterranean was already known to the Romans.

An even more striking similarity, is the days on which Viking and Roman gods were celebrated. The day of worship of Tyr was Tuesday, the same day as the worship of the Roman god Mars. The Latin name for the day after is Mercoledi, Miercoles, related to Mercury. The equivalent god in Viking mythology was Wodanaz, which is why the day is called Wednesday in English. The next day is the day of the thunder god: the Viking Thor for Thursday, the Roman Jupiter for Giovedi or Jueves. The day of the goddess of love, sex, and war was next. Because she was called Freyia in northern countries the day was called Friday or Freitag. In Latin countries where the goddess was called Venus, the day became Venerdi or Viernes.

But cultural similarities do not end there. The Vikings also used seers, which they called Volva. They practised human sacrifices, like the Cypriots. When they died they needed a boat to go to heaven, just like the Egyptians. That is why they buried their people by burning a boat or burying them in a grave shaped like a boat.

The story of the seven dwarfs is also from Germanic mythology. The stories were recollected by the Grimm brothers in 1812 as a collection of fairy tales. The story is so old that you can still see some of the Cypriot mythology within the story. The seven dwarfs were the creatures that helped Hephaestus in his mines. But the similarities do not end there. The evil queen keeps asking the question of 'who is the fairest of them all'—the same question that was present at the judgement of Paris when the golden apple was thrown between Hera, Athena, and Aphrodite marked 'to the fairest'. Even the apple stayed in the myth.

British Atlanteans

The Neolithic arrived through the Danube to the area of modern-day Denmark, but it did not stop there. Some moved to the area of what is now France, and they would become the Francs. The Viking Rollo became the first Duke of Normandie. The name Norman shows their origin, as it meant people of the north. The same Norse man would give us the name Norway.

The Normans invaded the island of Britain in 1066, completing the colonization of north and west Europe by Germanic tribes. But when the Normans invaded, the island of Britain was already Viking. It was not because of the Viking raids that started at the end of the 8th century AD. The actual inhabitants of the British Isles were, and had been for many years, of the same origin. Angles and Saxons had been there for more than a century. Both Angles and Saxons were tribes that arrived from the area of modern-day Denmark during the period after the Roman occupation. It is from the Danish term 'Angeln' that we have the name of the country, England.

The arrival of the first Neolithic culture in Britain occurred around 4000 BC. This would be the people that actually built Stonehenge. The same Neolithic people that built Cyclopean structures all around the Mediterranean.

In the 12th-century, Geoffrey of Monmouth wrote History of the Kings of Britain in which he gives the origin of the inhabitants of the island. The book was believed to have been the history of Britain from their first inhabitants. In it he tells us that the island was first inhabited by a race of giants.

Could it be that the giants that he talks about are the same as the giants of the Gigantomachy?

The giants that lived in Anatolia and the ones that arrived in Britain could have been the same. Geoffrey of Monmouth tells us that the first inhabitants were ruled by Brutus of Troy. It was Brutus from whom he believed the British got their name. Brutus arrived and founded a city called New Troy. Troy Nova would become Trinovantum. Trinovantum would become the city of London:

'When he came to the river Thames, he walked its banks and found the very spot for his plans. There he founded a city which he called New Troy. It retained this name for a long time until it was eventually corrupted to Trinovantum. When Lud, the brother of Cassibellaunus, who fought against Julius Caesar, came to the throne, he surrounded the city with fine walls and wonderfully built towers; and he commanded that it be named Kaerlud or Lud; s city. Afterwards this was the cause of a mighty argument between him and his brother Nennius, who was indignant that Lud wish to suppress the name Troy in the realm...

... After Brutus had built his city, he furnished it with dwellers to inhabit it lawfully and establish a code under which they could live in peace. At this time the priest Eli was ruling Judea and the Ark

of the Covenant had been captured by the Philistines. The sons of Hector were ruling at Troy after the descendants of Antenor were exiled. In Italy there ruled the third of the Latins, Silvius Aeneas, the son of Aeneas and the uncle of Brutus.'

Irish Atlanteans

Ireland's origin seems also related to the Danaids. The Lebor Gabála Érenn, or Book of the Invasions, describes the origin of the Irish people through the different invasions. The last of these was the invasion by the Gaels from the Iberian Peninsula. They were the sons of Mil (also known as Milesius), whose people inhabited Miletus in western Turkey. According to the legend, the ultimate ancestor of the Gaels was a Scythian king whose descendants settled in Hispania. Scythians were inhabitants of the area from the northern Black Sea all the way to Iran. But the story started with the Tuath Dé (Tribe of the Gods), a race of supernaturally gifted people. Part of the group includes a goddess of love and beauty who came from the island of Tir Tairngire ('the land of promise'). This group later became known as the Tuatha Dé Danann (Tribe of the goddess Danu). The Danaids seem to appear in all early European mythology. The Irish version, according to their myth, occurred around 1800 BC.

Another Irish myth also relates them to the descendants of Kittim, the same people who descended from Noah. According to the myth, Nemed arrived in Ireland in 2320 BC. He was the son of Agnoman of Scythia, Agnoman being the son of Piamp, son of Tait, son of Sera, son of Sru, son of Esru, son of Friamaint, son of Fathochta, son of Magog, son of Japheth, son of Noah. The Muintir Nemid set sail from the Caspian Sea in 44 ships, but after a year and a half of sailing, the only ship to reach Ireland was Nemed's.

This genealogy seems to agree with the idea that the Irish were Scythians, as Josephus wrote:

'Magog founded those that from him were called Magogites, but who are by the Greeks called Scythians.'

This group of people reached Ireland after the previous race, which was believed to have come from Mygdonia, an area of Thrace, had already died out. Legend holds that that group had arrived in Ireland a few years after the flood.

The influence of the Danaids in European mythology is not surprising as we all have the same origin, as seen from DNA research that dates the movement of the people from the island of Cyprus reaching the rest of Europe. It is obvious that their myths, gods and traditions would travel with them.

Asian Atlanteans

But the influence of Atlantean culture does not stop there. As we know, that same common linguistic origin does not just end in Europe. After all, the languages are called Indo-European, so there should be some evidence of the same mythology in ancient India.
Is there any evidence of the Danaids in India?

The same Danu that appears in Ireland also appears in Vedic traditions. Danu in India is a water goddess. Danu had many sons called Danava. They were related to water, just as the Danaids or the Denyens were. Related to water like the Donau River or the Danes all descendant of the same Dan or Danaus.

Indians also have a story of a great flood. In the Indian version it is Manu and Matsya who are the main characters of a legend that

appears around 700 BC. Matsya (the incarnation of Lord Vishnu as a fish) forewarns Manu (a human) about an impending catastrophic flood and orders him to collect all the grains of the world in a boat. In some forms of the story, all living creatures are also to be preserved in the boat. When the flood destroys the world, Manu – in some versions accompanied by the seven great sages – survives by boarding the ark, which Matsya pulls to safety. Both the idea of the seven sages and the animals and the flood are very similar to Greek mythology.
The story of Adonis and Aphrodite is retold in the story of Krishna. Krishna is always depicted as a young boy, and his death is similar to that of Adonis—Adonis killed by a boar and Krishna killed by an arrow in a hunting accident.

The leader of all the Devas (gods) is Indra, the god of thunderstorm, just like Zeus. The word Deva derived from the same Indo-European word for god Deus, Theo, Dio.

The fact that the gods in Indian mythology appear to be blue, might have a very Mediterranean reason. The rulers were known to wear the Tyrian blue clothing. The clothing made of the Murex sea snail would become the colour linked to the Phoenicians. The same blue dye that has been found in 4,000-year-old silk from the Pyrgo-Mavroraki site just outside Limassol.

Even the story of Achilles can be found in India's mythology. In the Iliad, Thetis, the sea goddess, fears her son will go to war and be killed. In the Mahabharata, the river goddess Ganga, gives birth to Bhishma, who becomes the hero of the Mahabharata war but is killed by arrows, just like Achilles. Achilles is called a Kouros, and Bhishma is the son of king Kuru. The stories are strikingly similar.

That the Cypriots reached all the way to the Indus Valley seems very reasonable, as this is the reason that the languages are called Indo-European. In book 13 of the Dionysiaca, Nonnus writes about the war with the Indians. You should not be surprised then when the Indus

Valley civilization that developed around the Indus river between 3300–1800 BC seemed to mirror the advances of the Cypriots. They had a very developed copper industry. They had a script that resembled that of the ancient Cypriot. They developed wells. They had very advanced water sanitation. There have even been suggestions that they were ruled by various kings, with people on an equal status. In religion they had gods that had very sexual representations. These gods were worshipped using baths and water, very similar to the worship of Aphrodite and Adonis.

The worship of Zeus, or more precisely the mountain of Zeus, was also present in India. The conical shape of the Cypriot Mount Olympus, or Stavrovouni would be worshipped around the world in many cultures. Every mountain that has the same shape as Stavrovouni seems to be a sacred mountain. Mount Kilimanjaro, Mount Fuji, Mount Ararat, Machapuchare in Nepal, Mount Teide, and Mount Kailash are just a few examples. When these mountains are near inhabited places, they become places of worship.

But there are some areas that are known for their plains. These areas are exactly where humans started to develop replacements for the sacred mountains. The most famous are the pyramids in Egypt. The oldest known pyramid in Egypt, is the Pyramid of Djoser dated to around 2650 BC. But there are older pyramids around the world. In Iran there is the Tepe Sialk ziggurat. The ziggurat follows a similar setting as Mount Olympus, where there would be the temple at the top of the mount. The oldest known one is dated to around 3000 BC. These same structures are found in many other areas. In Nubia, modern Sudan, there are more than 500 pyramids. The area was called the kingdom of Kush and was developed after the collapse of the Bronze Age. One of the most important sites in the area is the Al-Kurru site, where tombs of the Nubian royal family were found. Pyramids are also found in India, China, Indonesia, Cambodia and elsewhere, dating from 400 BC right up until 1,000 years ago. They are all built to house a temple or a tomb, just like the ziggurats and the Egyptian pyramids.

All seem to follow the same shape as Mount Olympus (Stavrovouni) of Cyprus, though there might even be evidence of pyramids in Cyprus. As Savvas Papadopoulos pointed out in Salamis of Paphos, there are many structures shaped like pyramids all over the island that have not been studied yet.

Further away you find pyramids in China which would suggest that the same people arrived in that area. And the evidence is not just the pyramids. A mummy of a woman was found and dated to around 1000 BC, but the woman was not Chinese or even Egyptian. The mummy had white skin, European features and red hair. The colour of the hair could have been achieved with a natural dye. The Henna plant used in Indian tattoos was used as a hair colouring during antiquity. In Cyprus, the Henna plant was widely used as a red hair dye up until the last century. The name of that plant was called Cypperus, clearly linking it to Cyprus. It is not surprising that it was used as a tattoo in India during weddings as part of a fertility ritual.

American Atlanteans

The issue with the pyramids as evidence of Atlantean influence is that there were also pyramids in South America. Could it be that the ancient migrants arrived in America well before Colombus or the Vikings?

The knowledge of a transoceanic continent seems to be confirmed by Isidoro of Seville (556–636 AD) when he wrote in the Etymologiae: 'Extra tres autem partes orbis quarta pars trans Oceanum interior est in meridie' (Apart from the three parts of the world (Europe, Africa and Asia), there is another continent in the other side of the Ocean). There is also quite a lot of physical evidence to support this. In the Deir-El-Bahari Necropoli in Thebes, a 3,000-year-old mummy named Henut Taui was discovered. The name of the mummy is translated as the lady of the two lands. What two lands they referred to was not clear. But in 1992 Svetlana Balabanova found that the mummy had traces of cocaine, hashish and nicotine. Cocaine and nicotine did not exist anywhere outside America. It seems when she was called 'lady of the two lands,' one of them might have been America. Tobacco residue was also found in many other mummies, including Ramesses II.

Could it be that someone from Egypt travelled to America? It seems clear that someone did do the trip. Mummies with cocaine and pyramids in America seem to point towards a cultural exchange between the two. But the mummies are Egyptian and not Cypriot. Is there any evidence that non-Egyptian people undertook the journey? In Brazil, there is a place called Bay of Jars, where amphorae have been found over the last 150 years.

Near Mexico City, a terracotta head of a man with European characteristics was found. Experts believed the clay figurine of a bearded man to be of 2nd-century Roman style.

A text discovered in the 17th century AD near the town of Paraiba (Brazil) had an inscription believed to be Phoenician. The text was translated and reads:

> 'We are children of Canaan from Sidon of the Eastern Kingdom of Merchants and are cast, I pray, here beside a central land of mountains (with this) offered choice gift to the Most High Gods and Goddesses in year 19 of King Hiram, I pray (still) strong, from the valley of Ezion-geber of the Red Sea. Thereby (we) journeyed with 10 ships and we were at sea together assuredly two years around the land of Ham. We were separated by the hand of Baal and no longer remained among our companions, I pray, we have come here, 12 men and 3 women at this new land. Devoted, I make, even whom men of wealth bow the knee, a pledge to the Most High Gods and Goddesses (with) sure hope.'

Despite the remoteness of the site of Paraiba, it would make sense to find an inscription in that area of Brazil as it is where the crossing to America would have been the shortest distance.

Unsurprisingly, it is claimed that such evidence are hoaxes created in modern times. Archaeologists find it very difficult to believe that there would be an ancient civilization that would have travelled the distance and not left any trace. But even if you believe that all this could be fake, there is within the myths of the ancient inhabitants of America suggestions of the arrival of 'white people'.

First, we have all the texts regarding the arrival of Colombus and how the indigenous believed them to be 'the second coming of the gods'. In Incan society, Viracocha was a white god related to the sea. He was the creator of all things and the god of the sun and thunder. He was also depicted holding thunderbolts in his hands. Pedro Sarmiento de Gamboa, the 16th-century explorer and historian, noted that Viracocha was described as 'a man of medium height, white and dressed in a white robe like an alb secured round the waist, and that he carried a staff and a book in his hands'.

Could it be that Viracocha was the Incan interpretation of Zeus? It is strange that he was depicted holding a book in his hand as the Incas did not have a written language. He was believed to be the god that sent the flood to destroy men.

In the Paracas peninsula there is a massive glyph believed to depict a trident or the lightning rod of Viracocha.

Fig. 6.3: Paracas trident.[91]

Even more connections can be made in Central America. In Mexico there is a large carved stele dating from around 300 BC called Izapa Stela 5. The stele depicts what is believed to be a creation myth. The scene seems to show a tree being carried over water. The sacred tree is quite similar to images depicting the worship of Apollo.

Indigenous cultures also use masks just like the Cypriots did. Masks have been found in Mayan Olmec and Aztec sites. All of them seem to represent the gods.

But the most striking resemblance is that of Quetzalcoatl. Just as Adonis, he had a virgin conception, a premature violent death and was expected to resurrect. When the Spanish arrived, they were believed to be the resurrected Quetzalcoatl. Hernan Cortez was depicted as Quetzalcoatl on many representations.

Quetzalcoatl was the god that gave them corn and taught them to read the stars. The Mayan calendar has 13 days, and Quetzalcoatl's day was always number nine representing wind. But day nine was also the day of fertility, war and the planet Venus. No surprise that Quetzalcoatl was the representation of planet Venus and the symbol of death and resurrection, and that he favoured human sacrifice.

North America is not exempt from evidence of the arrival of those same people either. Berkley, Massachusetts, is where the so-called Dighton rock is located. Carved into the rock are many ancient petroglyphs including boats that resemble Viking or ancient Greek ships. Petroglyphs of boats appear in many parts of the world, some of them in North America, some in South America, but also in Sweden. It all seems to suggest that the same people that colonized Europe and carved the glyphs, did travel to America much earlier than previously thought.

In the area of the Great Lakes, there is another site that appears to contradict the conventional theory of the Spanish conquest of America. It may even challenge the Viking discovery of America.

The area has copper mines, even though most native cultures did not use copper. The mine complex is vast. The estimate is that around 50,000 tons of copper was extracted in the area. The actual purity of the metal is very high, only matched by Cypriot copper. The dating of the copper mines is also quite revealing. From the research done on the site it is believed that the mines were used from around 2500 BC. No culture in the whole American continent used copper during that time. It therefore seems no surprise that the abandonment of the mines occurred abruptly in 1200 BC—the exact date of the end of the Bronze Age and the date of the Atlantis disaster.

It looks like the people of Atlantis arrived in America well before 2500 BC, roughly 4,000 years before Colombus. A crossing of the ocean by the people of Atlantis would certainly explain why we call it the

Atlantic Ocean.

A possible confirmation was found in a field in 1896 near Newberry. A farmer trying to uproot an old tree trunk to plough his field made a strange discovery. Among the roots he found an ancient artefact; a stone tablet with some strange writings resembling hieroglyphs. They were studied and found not to match any known language. They were soon believed to be fake and were put in storage. But in 1909, a new development occurred. In Cyprus some ancient script was discovered that resembled the script of Crete. But it was not the same. The new language was labeled Cypro-Minoan. Many years later the script in the Newberry tablet was re-examined and found to be written in the Cypro-Minoan script, the language of Cyprus from 1600 BC until 1100 BC. The dates seem to accord, as that was the language used in Cyprus at the time when the Great Lakes copper mines were in use.

The arrival of the ancient Cypriots in America would also coincide with another mythological and astrological event in South America. One of the creations of the god Quetzalcoatl was the calendar. It is logical to arrive at the conclusion that when Quetzalcoatl arrived in South America, he would give them the calendar and start counting from that point. This gives us the date of the discovery of America by the Cypriots as 3114 BC.

Pacific Atlanteans

But the Atlantean travels did not stop there. The god Viracocha, after giving the Incas their civilization, would then disappear west to the Pacific Ocean. That a journey must have been made much earlier than previously thought has already been established, because American plant species like the sweet potato were already known in Polynesia well before the arrival of Europeans in the 15th century AD.

If the people from Atlantis were the ones that made that journey, it would be no surprise then that the myth of the flood was also known in such remote areas as the Hawaiian isles, where the myth goes that a man called Nu'u built a boat to escape from the great flood.

But the idea that the ancient Cypriots travelled around the earth should not surprise us. It was a Cypriot who did the measurements that Aristotle mentions in De Caelo:

> 'Indeed there are some stars seen in Egypt and in the neighbourhood of Cyprus which are not seen in the northerly regions; and stars, which in the north are never beyond the range of observation, in those regions rise and set. All of which goes to show not only that the earth is circular in shape, but also that it is a sphere of no great size: for otherwise the effect of so slight a change of place would not be so quickly apparent. Hence one should not be too sure of the incredibility of the view of those who conceive that there is continuity between the parts about the pillars of Hercules and the parts about India, and that in this way the ocean is one. As further evidence in favour of this they quote the case of elephants, a species occurring in each of these extreme regions, suggesting that the common characteristic of these extremes is explained by their continuity. Also, those mathematicians who try to calculate the size of the earth's circumference arrive at the figure 400,000 stades. This indicates not only that the earth's mass is spherical in shape, but also that as compared with the stars it is not of great size.'[92]

The fact that the measurements he mentions were taken in Cyprus and Egypt clearly shows that it was Cypriots and Egyptians making the measurements and studies. If it had been the Greeks making the studies, he would clearly use Greek places to refer to the measurements. He also noted that the shape of the earth must be round as that was the shape shown on the moon's surface during eclipses, making Cypriots and Egyptians the first to challenge flat-earthers.

CONCLUSION

The importance of Atlantis might have been exaggerated due to the mystery of the text and its unknown location, but one can clearly realise that the historical importance of the island of Cyprus has been neglected and underestimated.

If you believe the story written by Plato, the events at the dawn of civilization would be as follows:
In 9500 BC, a group of adventurers decided to use bundles of reeds, probably glued together with bitumen, to make the first seafaring boat. In that boat they went to investigate the piece of land that they could see from the top of Mount Aqraa in Syria. The island they found looked far different from how it does today. The island was a vast forest covered with huge oak and cedar trees. The weather was much milder than on the mainland. The winters were not as cold and the summers not as hot thanks to the surrounding sea. The trees caught the humidity from the sea and the rivers were full of water.

Agriculture thrived in Cyprus with more crops produced per year than any other known area. The animals that these first settlers brought with them did not find any natural predators and began to reproduce rapidly. Soon the people there found that tasks that used to take all year took very little time in Cyprus. Crops seemed to take care of themselves and finding animals to hunt was never a problem. It was like living in paradise. That gave the people of Cyprus a major advantage that none of the people that lived in Mesopotamia, Syria or Anatolia had: free time. With free time, the people started thinking of ways to improve their lives. They created wells to make the farming even easier. They introduced cats to prey on vermin. Soon they decided to build better ships and explore other lands. Wherever they went they shared their knowledge, improving the standards of living of people around the globe. Cypriots were, and still are, very generous people. They went with their boats to all European lands, spreading the most impactful development in history: agriculture. It is from this time that we can trace a common given language from Europe to India.

These early Cypriots lived in settlements like Chirokitia. They fashioned stones from all over the island into tools. They started to collect copper and soon found that under the earth lay an endless supply of it. The demand from civilizations on the mainland for this new material created their first trading network. Their wealth, ingenuity, and dominance of the sea took them all around the world. It is during those travels that the Cypriots confirmed that the Earth was round, something so difficult to believe that in Europe people were still being killed for suggesting such a concept 4,000 years later. During one of their trading missions, they found out that adding tin to their metal resulted in an incredibly hard material, ideal for making stronger tools and, most importantly, the first bronze weapons.

People from around the world started to see that the Cypriot people had an edge they could only dream of. They started to consider them the representatives of gods, and Cypriot priest/kings began to wear masks to accentuate their difference from other cultures. Neighbouring peoples from all over the Fertile Crescent started to worship at Cypriot shrines and make pilgrimages to the island. The island was divided between the ten gods, just as Plato said. Each of the ten areas was to be ruled by a king, just as Plato said, that would also serve as the god's head priest. Paphos became the richest town in the world and a centre of pilgrimage, with women visiting the town to offer their virginity to the goddess. The king of Paphos, rivalled only by King Midas, had so much money that they could send tons of metal and other products as presents to the pharaohs. It is at that point that the town built on a little island inside a lake in the Larnaka Salt Lake started to thrive. It is that town that Plato talks about when he says that they had no worries about material things.

Since this island of the gods was producing the most precious metal of the age, everyone wanted to control it. Previously subservient countries started to use bronze tools to try to gain the upper hand over the Cypriots. The Titans of Anatolia would claim control of the island, as would the Egyptians of Tutmose III. After the 1450 BC tsunami that hit Cyprus, the Mycenaeans took the opportunity to gain some power and become nearly independent from Cypriots. Through marriage, the rulers of Mycenae took control of some sites on the island. Their fate was sealed when a Mycenaean ruler killed Aphrodite's lover in a hunting accident. It got to the point where something had to be done. A big battle between the Hittites and Egyptians managed to weaken both kingdoms without giving either of them the upper hand. The remaining nine kingdoms decided that the time had arrived.

When the newly married Helen went to fulfil her duties at the temple of Aphrodite, the goddess gave her to the son of the ruler of Troy. Menelaos took offense believing it was an attack on his kingdom and as such he requested the support of all the other members of the ten kingdoms (as it was written in the Pillars of Orichalcum in Atlantis) in order to destroy the offenders, which led to a war that took ten years, and that would be called by some the Titanomachy. Once the Titans were destroyed, it was time to destroy the Egyptians. The attempt did not go as planned and the Egyptian kingdom did survive, but it was so damaged that it would never regain the strength it had at the time of Rameses. The non Mycenean kingdoms though they had to punish the people that started the war and prepared to destroy them. But the wife of Agamemnon had already taken measures to ensure that Agamemnon would not reign when they got back from the war. Once that was achieved, settlements that belonged to Mycenaeans who resisted the change of ruler were destroyed. In Greece all the settlements were abandoned, and the warriors who returned from the Trojan War decided to settle back on Cyprus. Greece would go back to the Stone Age with little to show in terms of civilization.

Cyprus received a devastating blow with another tsunami that levelled most of the coastal sites, especially the biggest and most developed city in the country. The site was abandoned, and the surviving inhabitants would settle in the nearby area of Phoenicia. The rest would settle in the towns that the rulers of the newly arrived Greek refugees had created. Once these cities grew, it became time for the Cypriots and the Phoenicians to search for new countries in which to settle. All the cities in Greece started to develop after 900 BC. A bit later cities were founded in Italy and northern Africa. Soon the whole Mediterranean would be colonized.

When the 8th century BC started, it seemed clear that the survivors of the Titans would seek revenge. It was then that a migration towards Greece started. That period saw the orientalisation of Greece. With that migration the people started to feel the need to keep their traditions and stories of the past alive, and that they needed to be recorded in order for them not to be lost. It was then that the people that settled in Greece decided to use the alphabet developed in Cyprus during the Greek Dark Ages, the Phoeniki Grammata. Those letters allowed them to record the stories of their past. While the Cypriots took the language to Greece, the Phoenicians took it to the Middle East. All the languages around the Mediterranean from the early Middle Ages descend from the two languages.

CONCLUSION

Around 720 BC, the Giants (the Assyrians) started their attempt to avenge the Titans. It is then that they took control of the island of Cyprus and left a stele to commemorate the moment. A great number of inhabitants of Cyprus moved away from their homeland. The gods had to find a new home. All but Aphrodite left the island and settled around Greece. There were many attempts to fight back against the Perses, or Assyrians. The Ionian revolt was the best-known example. But they did not succeed. It was not until the Persians reached mainland Greece that the Greek luck changed. Battles like the famous Marathon became the turning point. But it would not be until Alexander the Great, that the Greeks would regain control of the area controlled by the people of Atlantis. It cannot be a coincidence that Alexander decided to turn around the moment he arrived at the furthest extent of the Indo-European language.

For sure Atlantis is not the superpower that it once was. Yet it has still had a profound influence on everyone on the entire planet. The influence is even greater if you are in any of the areas where the Indo-European languages have developed. Even more so if you live in any of the European countries. But if you live in Cyprus or just visiting, you can take pride in knowing that you are on the island described by Plato centuries ago, the island of Atlantis.

BIBLIOGRAPHY

- Plato (360 BC): "Timaeus" Trans. Benjamin Jowett (1871) C. Scribner's Sons.

- Plato (360 BC): "Critias" Trans. Benjamin Jowett (1871) C. Scribner's Sons.

- Drews, Robert: "The end of the bronze age, Changes in warfare and the catastrophe CA. 1200 B.C." (1993) Princeton University Press.

- Gladstone, William E.: "Studies on Homer and the Homeric Age. Vol.1 Prolegomena, Achaeis or the Ethnology of the Greek Races." (1858) Oxford University Press.

- Gladstone, William E.: "Studies on Homer and the Homeric Age. Vol.2 Olympus Or the Religion Of The Homeric Age." (1858) Oxford University Press.

- Gladstone, William E.: "Studies on Homer and the Homeric Age. Vol.3 Agore, Ilios, Thalassa and Aoidos" (1858) Oxford University Press.

- Frazer, James G.: "Adonis, Attis, Osiris; Studies in the history of Oriental Religion." (1906) MacMillan and Co., Limited. London.

- Ohnefalsch-Richter, Max Hermann: "Kypros, The Bible and Homer: Oriental Civilization, Art and Religion in Ancient Times" Vol 1-2 (1893) Asher & Co. Bedford Street, Covent Garden, London.

- Burkert, Walter: "The Orientalizing Revolution. Near Eastern Influence on Greek Culture in the Early Archaic Age." Trans. Margaret Pinder & Water Burkert. (1992) Harvard University Press.

- Wood, Michael: "In Search of the Trojan War" (1985) BBC Books.

- Archimandrita Kyprianou. "Cronological History of the island of Cyprus" 3rd edition 2001 K. Epifaniou

- Kilgour, Henry: "The Hebrew of Iberian Race; Including the Pelasgians, The Phoenicians, The Jews, The British, And Others" (1872) Trubner & Co.

- Homer (8th Century BC): "The Iliad" Trans. Martin Hammond (1987) Penguin Classics.

- Homer (8th Century BC): "The Odyssey" Trans. E.V. Rieu (1946) Penguin Classics.

- Herodotus (5th Century BC): "The Histories" Trans. Robin Waterfield. (1998) Oxford University Press.

- Apollodorus (2-1st Century BC): "The library of Greek Mythology" Trans. Robin Hard. (1997) Oxford Univesity Press.

- Hesiod (8-7th Century BC): "Theogony and Works and Days" Trans. M.L. West (1988) Oxford Univesity Press.

- Virgil (1st Century BC): "The Aeneid" Trans. David West (1990) Penguin Classics.

- Aeschylus. Prometheus Bound and Other Plays. Trans. Philip Vellacott. Penguin Classics.

- William of Tyre, A History of Deeds Done Beyond the Sea. Translated, and Annotated by Emily Atwater Babcock and A. C. Krey. Columbia University Press 1943

- Sarmast, Robert: "Discovery of Atlantis; The startling case for the island of Cyprus." (2006) First source Publications.

- Sherwood Fox, W. "Aphrodite: Mother Earth. John Hopkins University Press. American Journal of Philology. Vol 41. N3 (1920) pp 283-286

- "Sources for the History of Cyprus. Vol 1 Greek and Latin texts to the third century A.D." Edited by Wallace and Orphanides (1990) Institute of Cypriot Studies, University At Albany and Cyprus College; Konos Press.

- "Sources for the History of Cyprus. Vol 2 Near Eastern and Aegean Texts from the third to the first Millennia BC" Edited by A. Bernard Knapp (1996) Greek and Cyprus Research Center.

- "Sources for the History of Cyprus. Vol VII Greek Texts of the Fourth to Thirteenth Centuries" Hans A. Pohlsander University at Albany,

BIBLIOGRAPHY

State University of New York. Greece and Cyprus Research Center 1999.

- Hesiod (8-7th Century BC): "The shield, Catalogue of women and other fragments." Trans. Glenn W. Most (2007) Loeb classic library, Harvard University Press.

- Nonnos (5th Century AD) Dionysiaca Trans. W.H.D. Rouse (1940) Loeb classic library, Harvard University Press.

- "Bible. The CTS New Catholic" (2007) Catholic Truth Society.

- Pausanias (2nd Century AD): "Description of Greece, Volume IV, Books 8.22-10: Arcadia, Boeotia, Phocis and Ozolian Locri." (1935) Loeb Classical Library.

- Hala Sultan Tekke. Excavations 1897-1971 Paul Astrom. 1976 Paul Astrom Forlag

- Geoffrey of Monmouth (12th Century AD): Trans. Neil Wright (2007) The Boydell Press.

- Papageorgiou, Costas: "Cypriot Mythology" Trans. Despina Pirketti (2004) Parga Publications.

- Papadopoulos, Savvas: "Salamis of Paphos, testimonies and theories" (2008) Imprinta Ltd.

- Powell, Barry B.: "Homer and the origin of the Greek alphabet" (1991) Cambridge University Press.

- Belgiorno, Maria Rosaria: "A coppersmith tomb of early-middle bronze age in Pyrgos (Limassol) (1997) Department of antiquities, Cyprus.

- Peltenburg, Edgar: "figures in a bowl. Evidence of Chalcolithic religion from Kissonerga Mosphilia (PlateI-II)"

- Hill, George: "A History of Cyprus" (1940) Cambridge University Press.

- Schneider, Tammi (Editor): "The Philistines and other 'Sea Peoples' in Text and Archaeology" (2013) The society of Biblical Literature.

- Boardman, John (Editor): "The Cambridge Ancient History. Vol III. The expansion of the Greek world, Eight to Sixth century B.C." (1982) Cambridge University Press.

- Steel, Louise: "The Social World of Early-Middle Bronze Age Cyprus: Rethinking the Vounous Bowl" (2013) Journal of Mediterranean Archaeology 26.1 51-73

- Fischer, Peter M.: "The new Swedish Cyprus expedition 2010 Excavations at Dromolaxia Vizatzia / Hala Sultan Tekke. Preliminary results.

- Walcek Averett, Erin: "Masks and Ritual Performance on the Island of Cyprus" (Jan 2015) American Journal of Archaeology Vol. 119, No. 1, pp. 3-45

- Rollin, Charles: "The ancient history of the Egyptians, Carthaginians, Assyrians, Babylonians, Medes and Persians, Macedonians, and Grecians" (1768)

- Hogarth, David George: "Ionia and the East: Six Lectures Delivered Before the University of London" (1909) Cambridge University Press.

- Sakellarios, Athanasios: "Ta Kypriaka" (1855)

- Donnelly, Ignatius: "Atlantis, the Antediluvian World" (1976) Dover Publications.

- Luce, J.V.: "Lost Atlantis: New Light on an Old Legend" (1969) McGraw-Hill.

- Butler, Samuel: "The Humour of Homer and other Essays" (1917) (2011) The floating Press.

- Frame, Douglas: "New Light on the Homeric Question: The Phaeacians Unmasked" (2012) http://chs.harvard.edu/CHS/article/display/4453

- Strabo (1st Century A.D.): "The Geography of Strabo" Trans. Hans Claude Hamilton (1892) H. G. Bohn.

- Burkert, Walter: "Greek Religion" (1985) Basil Blackwell Publisher and Harvard University Press.

- Carleton Stevens Coon, "The Story of Man", New York, Knopf, 1954

- Pliny the Elder (1st century AD): "Natural History" Trans. John Bostock (1828) Baldwin and Cradock.

- Miczak, Marie Analkee: "Henna's Secret history: The history, mystery & folklore of Henna" (2001) Writers Club Press.

- Vigne, Jean-Denis: "The Origins of Mammals on the Mediterra nean Islands as an Indicator of Early Voyaging" Proceedings of the Wenner Gren Workshop held at Reggio Calabriaon October 19-21, 2012 Island Archaeology and the origins of Seafaring in the Eastern Mediterranean.

BIBLIOGRAPHY

- Vigne, Jean-Denis: "Early taming of the cat in Cyprus" (2004) Science 9 April: 259.

- "Epic of Gilgamesh" (18th Century BC): Trans. N Sandars (1973) Penguin Adult.

- McCartney, Carol: "Prehistoric Occurrences in the Randi State Forest: a preliminary report of the Rantidi Forest Project. (1999).

- Frazer, James: "The golden Bough: A Study in Magic and Religion" (1922) The MacMillan Co. NY.

- Vigne, Jean-Denis: "Pre-Neolithic Wild Boar Management and Introduction to Cyprus more than 11400 years ago" (2009) Proc. Natl Acad Sci USA, Sept 22, 106(38) 16135–16138.

- Swiny, Stuart: "The earliest Prehistory of Cyprus: From Colonization to Exploitation" (2001) American Schools of Oriental Research.

- Wells S.A.: "American Drugs in Egyptian Mummies" Retrived (Feb2015) http://www.faculty.ucr.edu/~legneref/ethnic/mummy.htm

- Radner, Karen: "The stele of Sargon II of Assyria at Kition: A focus for an emerging Cypriot identity?" (2010) Interkulturalität in der Alten Welt. Harrassowitz Verlag Wiesbaden.

- Tertullian (2nd Century AD): "On the veiling of Virgins" Translated by S. Thelwall. From Ante-Nicene Fathers, Vol. 4. Edited by Alexander Roberts, James Donaldson, and A. Cleveland Coxe. (Buffalo, NY: Christian Literature Publishing Co.

- Peltenburg, E. J: "Neolithic Revolution: new perspectives on southwest Asia in light of recent discoveries in Cyprus" (2004) Oxbow books.

- Gaudet, John: "Papyrus: The Plant That Changed the World – From Ancient Egypt to Today's Water Wars" (2014) Pegasus Books LLC.

- Belgiorno, Maria Rosaria: "New Suggestions from Pyrgos/Mavrorachi on Cypriote 2000 B.C. proto-industria Society and its Gender Perspective" (2008) in Fond and Results from the Swdish Cyprus Expedition, 1927–1931, Stockholm.

- Taylor, Isaac: "The Alphabet; An Account of the Origin and Development of Letters" (1883) Kegan Paul, Trench, & Co. London.

- Knapp, A. Bernard: "Alashiya, Caphtor/Keftiu, and Eastern Mediterranean Trade: Recent Studies in Cypriote Archaeology and History" Review Article (1985) Journal of Field Archaeology Vol.12

- *Bouckaert, Remco:* "Mapping the origins and expansion of the Indo-European language family" (2012) Science 337, 957 DOI: 10.1126/science.1219669

- *Fernández, Eva et al.* "Ancient DNA Analysis of 8000 B.C. Near Eastern Farmers Supports an Early Neolithic Pioneer Maritime Colonization of Mainland Europe through Cyprus and the Aegean Islands." Ed. Scott M. Williams. PLoS Genetics 10.6 (2014): e1004401. PMC. Web. 15 Feb. 2015.

- *Iacovou,Maria:* "The Greek Exodus to Cyprus: The Antiquity of Hellenism" (1999) Mediterranean Historical Review, 14(2) 1-28

- *Voskos, Ioannis and Knapp, Bernard:* "Cyprus at the End of the Late Bronze Age: Crisis and Colonization or Continuity and Hybridization?" (2008) American Journal of Archaeology. October (112.4)

- *Wachsmann, Shelley:* "The Ships of the Sea People" (1982) International Journal of Nautical and Underwater Exploration. 11.4: 297-304.

- *Sugimoto, David T.:* "Transformation of a Goddess; Ishtar – Astarte – Aphrodite" (2014) Academic Press Fribourg. Vandenhoeck & Ruprecht Gottingen.

- *Herva, Vesa-Pekka & Nordin, Jonas M.:* "Unearthing Atlantis and performing the past: Ancient things, alternative histories and the present past in the Baroque world" (2015) Journal of Social Archaeology February 2015 vol. 15 no. 1 116–135

- *D'Amato, Raffaele and Salimbeti, Andrea:* "Sea Peoples of the Bronze Age Mediterranean: c. 1400BC-1000BC (2015) Osprey Publishing Ltd.

ENDNOTES

1   Cassius Dio, Roman History, 68, 32 2-3.

2   Ibid.

3   William of Tyre, A History of Deeds Done Beyond the Sea. Translated, and Annotated by Emily Atwater Babcock and A. C. Krey. Columbia University Press 1943. p. 253

4   Ibid. p. 254

5   'Tsunamis: revealing the abyss of the deep', Cyprus Mail, March 20, 2011.

6   Oracula Sibyllina (2-3rd century ad) from 'Sources for the history of Cyprus' (1990) 1 SHC 269.

7   Ibid.

8   Map of fertile crescent' by Nafsadh – Map of fertile cresent. png. Licensed under GFDL via Wikimedia Commons.

9   Pindar (450 bc), Nemean Odes, Isthmian Odes, Fragments, tr. William H. Race, Loeb Classic Library, LCL 485, 1997, p. 89.

10 Herodotus, Histories, II.2, tr. Robin Waterfield, Oxford World's Classics, 2008, pp. 95-96.

11 Remco Bouckaert, 'Mapping the Origins and Expansion of the Indo-European Language Family' (2012) 337(6097) Science 957-960 DOI: 10.1126/science. 1219669.

12   Fernández E, Pérez-Pérez A, Gamba C, Prats E, Cuesta P, Anfruns J, et al. (2014) Ancient DNA Analysis of 8000 B.C. Near Eastern Farmers Supports an Early Neolithic Pioneer Maritime Colonization of Mainland Europe through Cyprus and the Aegean Islands. PLoS Genet 10(6): e1004401. https://doi.org/10.1371/journal.pgen.1004401 Figure 1. Map of the spread of Neolithic farming cultures in Europe. Shadings represent isochronous Neolithic archaeological cultures and black lines frontier zones between them. Analyzed sites in the Fertile Crescent are also located in the map. All dates are in years B.C.

13   Fernández E, Pérez-Pérez A, Gamba C, Prats E, Cuesta P, Anfruns J, et al. (2014) Ancient DNA Analysis of 8000 B.C. Near Eastern Farmers Supports an Early Neolithic Pioneer Maritime Colonization of Mainland Europe through Cyprus and the Aegean Islands. PLoS Genet 10(6): e1004401. https://doi.org/10.1371/journal. pgen.1004401
Figure 4. Contour map of Fst distances between the PPNB population and modern populations of the database. Only populations with clear geographic distribution were included. Gradients indicate genetic distance between the PPNB and the modern populations (dark: small; clear: high). https://doi:10.1371/journal.pgen.1004401.g004/ https://journals.plos.org/plosgenetics/article/figure/image?size=large&id=10.1371/journal.pgen.1004401.g004

14   Yorgos Facorellis (https://commons.wikimedia.org/wiki/File:Dispilio_signs.jpg), Dispilio signs", https://creativecommons.org/licenses/by/3.0/legalcode

15   https://www.britishmuseum.org/collection/object/W_1929-1012-1

16   M. Iacovou, 'Mapping the ancient kingdoms of Cyprus. Cartography and classical scholarship during the Enlightenment', in George Tolias and Dimitris Loupis (eds), Eastern Mediterranean Cartographies, Athens: Institute for Neohellenic Research, 2004, Tetradia Ergasias, pp. 25–26, 263–285 at p. 271.

17   Ibid. at p. 269; Strabo 14, 6.

18   Eustathios of Thessalonike (ca 1115–1195/96) Commentary on Illiad 23.826 (1332.3–6) SHC. Greek texts of the 4th–13th centuries, Hans A. Pohlsander, p. 35, Greece and Cyprus Research Center, 1999.

19   Plutarch, Greek and Roman Lives, tr. John Dryden, Dover Publications, 2001.

ENDNOTES

20 Archimandrita Kyprianou, Chronological History of the Island of Cyprus, Nicosia, 1788, K. Epiphaniou, 2001, tr. A. Pyrkettti.

21 It has been interpreted that Plato or someone before him in the chain of the oral or written tradition of the report accidentally changed the very similar Greek words for 'bigger than' ('meson') and 'between' ('mezon'): J.V. Luce, The End of Atlantis – New Light on an Old Legend, London, Thames and Hudson, 1969, p. 224.

22 Theodoret of Cyrrhus, Interpretatio in Ezechielem, 27.6, SHC. Greek texts of the 4th–13th centuries, Hans A. Pohlsander, p. 35, Greece and Cyprus Research Center, 1999.

23 Map created by Zacharias Archontous

24 Josephus, Antiquities of the Jews, 1.127–129, SHC, p. 164.

25 Pliny, HN 34.2-4, SHC, p. 146.

26 Aristotle, Mirabilia, 142, SHC, p. 53.

27 Pliny, HN 34.2-4, SHC, p. 147.

28 A. Bernard Knapp, Near Eastern and Aegean texts from the third to the first Millennia BC, SHC, p. 18.

29 Unknown Author (7-6th century bc), 'Homeric Hymns', tr. Jules Cashford, Penguin Classics, 2003.

30 Unknown Author (7-6th century bc), 'Homeric Hymns', tr. Jules Cashford, Penguin Classics, 2003.

31 Image created by Zacharias Archontous using Google Earth base image.

32 Image supplied and permission to publish granted by the Department of Antiquities, Cyprus.

33 Sources for the History of Cyprus, Vol. II, Near Eastern and Aegean texts from the Third to the First Millennia BC, Ugaritic Documents from Ugarit, p. 37.

34 Hesiod (8th century bc), Theogony, tr. M.L. West, Oxford World's Classics, 1999, pp. 8-9.

35 Image supplied and permission to publish granted by the Department of Antiquities, Cyprus.

36 Image supplied and permission to publish granted by the Department of Antiquities, Cyprus.

37 Image supplied and permission to publish granted by the Department of Antiquities, Cyprus.

38 Image supplied and permission to publish granted by the Department of Antiquities, Cyprus.

39 New York Times, February 12, 1911, p. 35.

40 Ibid.

41 Homer, Odyssey, Nausicaa-6.41–46, p. 77, tr. E.V. Rieu, Penguin Classics, 1946.

42 Homer, Odyssey, Circe-10.307–308, p. 133, tr. E.V. Rieu, Penguin Classics, 1946.

43 Hesiod,Theogony, pp. 564–566, p. 20, tr. M.L. West, Oxford World's Classics, 1988.

44 Samuel Butler (1774–1839) (https://commons.wikimedia.org/wiki/File:Armenia,_Colchis,_Iberia,_Albania,_Etc.jpg), Armenia, Colchis, Iberia, Albania, Etc", marked as public domain, more details on Wikimedia Commons: https://commons.wikimedia.org/wiki/Template:PD-Gutenberg

45 flydime (https://commons.wikimedia.org/wiki/File:Turquoise_Lake_Crater_-_Turkmenistan,_Darvaza_-_panoramio.jpg), „Turquoise Lake Crater - Turkmenistan, Darvaza - panoramio"

46 Strabo, Geography, Vol. VII, 16.2.7, Loeb Classical Library edition, 1932.

47 Map created by Zacharias Archontous

48 Maurice Bowra, Homer and His Forerunners, Nelson, Edinburgh, 1955, pp. 1–2.

49 Immanuel Velikovsky, The Dark Age in Asia Minor, retrieved February 2016 from www.varchive.org/dag/amdark.htm.

50 Emmet John Sweeney, Gods Heroes and Tyrants: Greek chronology in Chaos, Algora Publishing, 2009, p. 21.

51 Walter Burkert, The Orientalizing Revolution. Near Eastern Influence on Greek Culture in the Early Archaic Age, tr. Margaret Pinder & Water Burkert, Harvard University Press, 1992, p. 27.

52 Adversus Haereses or Panarion, 42.11.17, Elenchus 12b, tr. F. Williams, Epiphanios of Salamis, SHC,. Vol. VII, p. 10.

53 (1926) 20 Classical Quarterly.

54 H.G. Evelyn-White, Hesiod, Homeric Hymns, and Homerica. Web edition published by eBooks@Adelaide.

55 https://upload.wikimedia.org/wikipedia/commons/b/b9/Boars%27s_tusk_helmet_NAMA6568_Athens_Greece1.jpg

56 Maria Iacovou, 'The Greek Exodus to Cyprus: the antiquity of Hellenism' (1999) 14(2) Mediterranean Historical Review 14-2.1-28.

57 Michael Wood, In Search of the Trojan War, BBC Books, 1985, p. 224.

58 Jeffrey P. Emanuel, Cretan Lie and Historical Truth: Examining Odysseus' Raid on Egypt in Its Late Bronze Age Context, Centre for Hellenic Studies, Harvard University, 2020.

59 CTS New Catholic Bible, London, Incorporated Catholic Thruth Society, 2007, p. 232.

60 Homer, The Iliad, tr. Martin Hammond, Penguin Classics, 1987, p. 35, 2:651-694.

61 Rollin, Charles: "The ancient history of the Egyptians, Carthaginians, Assyrians, Babylonians, Medes and Persians, Macedonians, and Grecians" (1768). Oxford University Press. P159

62 Strabo, Geography. H.C. Hamilton, Esq., W. Falconer, M.A., Ed. 5.2.4. Iliad ii. 840 retrieved from https://www.perseus.tufts.edu/hopper/

63 Aeschylus. Prometheus Bound and Other Plays. Trans. Philip Vellacott. Penguin Classics. The Suppliants. P 57.

64 Gladstone, William E.: "Studies on Homer and the Homeric Age. Vol.1 Prolegomena, Achaeis or the Ethnology of the Greek Races." (1858) Oxford University Press. P. 190.

65 Ptolemy Hephaestion, New History Book 7 (summary from Photius, Myriobiblon 190) (trans. Pearse) (Greek mythographer C1st to C2nd A.D.) Retrieved from https://www.theoi.com/Cult/ApollonCult5.html

66 Homer, The Iliad, tr. Augustus Taber Murray, Loeb Classsic Library, 1924, p. 171.

67 Translated from Orichalcum

68 Hesiod, The Shield Catalogue of Women Other Fragments, tr. Glenn W. Most, Loeb Classic Library, 2007.

69 Gladstone, William E.: "Studies on Homer and the Homeric Age. Vol.1 Prolegomena, Achaeis or the Ethnology of the Greek Races." (1858) Oxford University Press. P. 191.

70 Aeschylus. Prometheus Bound and Other Plays. Trans. Philip Vellacott. Penguin Classics. Seven against Thebes. P 93

71 Amarna letter EA 147. Retrieved from: https://en.wikipedia.org/wiki/Amarna_letter_EA_147

72 Amarna letter EA 7. Retrieved from https://en.wikipedia.org/wiki/Amarna_letter_EA_7

73 Amarna letter EA 41 Retrieved from https://ancientegyptonline.co.uk/ea41/

74 Sources for the History of Cyprus, Volume II. Near Eastern and Aegean texts from the Third to the First Millennia BC. Akkadian Documents from Amarna. William L. Moran. P 22.

75 Sources for the History of Cyprus, Volume II. Near Eastern and Aegean texts from the Third to the First Millennia BC, Akkadian Document from Ugarit. Gary Beckman. P26.

76 Carleton Stevens Coon, The Story of Man, New York, Knopf, 1954.

77 Downloaded from https://www.clipart-history.com/picture.php?/4454. Author Egyptian Ideas of the Future Life By E. A. Wallis Budge Published in 1908. Available from www.gutenberg.org

78 Sources for the History of Cyprus, Volume II. Near Eastern and Aegean texts from the Third to the First Millennia BC, Akkadian Document from Babylon, Piotr Michalowski, p. 30.

79 Samuel Noah Kramer, The Sumerians: Their History, Culture, and Character, University of Chicago Press, 1963, p. 53.

ENDNOTES

80 Sources for the History of Cyprus, Volume VII. Greek texts of the fourth to thirteenth centuries. Choiroboskos, George. p. 77.

81 W. Sherwood Fox, 'Aphrodite: Mother Earth' (1920) 41(3) American Journal of Philology 283–286.

82 Scholia to Tzetzes, Historiae or Chiliades 1.86, SHC, Vol. VII, 'Greek text of the fourth to thrirteenth centuries', Hans A. Pohlsander, 1999, p. 173.

83 Epiphanios of Salamis, Adversus Haereses or Panarion, 30.25.8-9, SHC, Vol. VII, 'Greek text of the fourth to thrirteenth centuries', Hans A. Pohlsander, 1999.

84 Hyperides, Minor Attic Orators in two volumes, 2, with an English translation by J. O. Burtt, Harvard University Press, London, William Heinemann Ltd, 1962. Retrieved from www.perseus.tufts.edu.

85 David George Hogarth, Ionia and the East: Six Lectures delivered before the University of London 1909, Lecture 5, Cambridge University Press, 2012.

86 damian entwistle (https://commons.wikimedia.org/wiki/File:Carthage_National_Museum_representation_of_city.jpg), „Carthage National Museum representation of city", https://creativecommons.org/licenses/by-sa/2.0/legalcode

87 Apollodorus, The Library of Greek Mythology, 2.5.11, tr. Robin Hard, Oxford World's Classics, 2008, p. 82.

88 Ibid.

89 Pausanias, Description of Greece ix.41.2

90 (2015) 112(38) Proceedings of the National Academy of Sciences of the United States of America, September 22, pp. 11917–11922.

91 Alex Zanuccoli (https://commons.wikimedia.org/wiki/File:Paracas_Candelabra_-_Ica,_Peru.jpg), „Paracas Candelabra - Ica, Peru", https://creativecommons.org/licenses/by-sa/2.0/legalcode

92 Aristotle (384–322 BC) On the Heavens. Translated by J. L. Stocks. Book II. Chapter 14. Retrieved from: http://www.logoslibrary.org/aristotle/heavens/214.html

www.ingramcontent.com/pod-product-compliance
Lightning Source LLC
LaVergne TN
LVHW061613070526
838199LV00078B/7265